DATE DUE

MARTIAL ARTS FOR ATHLETIC CONDITIONING

MASTERING
Martial Arts

Mastering the Martial Arts Series

Judo: Winning Ways

Jujutsu: Winning Ways

Karate: Winning Ways

Kickboxing: Winning Ways

Kung Fu: Winning Ways

Martial Arts for Athletic Conditioning: Winning Ways

Martial Arts for Children: Winning Ways

Martial Arts for Women: Winning Ways

Ninjutsu: Winning Ways

Taekwondo: Winning Ways

Martial Arts for Athletic Conditioning

ERIC CHALINE

Series Consultant
Adam James
10th Level Instructor
Founder: Rainbow Warrior Martial Arts
Director: Natl. College of Exercise Professionals

MASON CREST
www.masoncrest.com

Mason Crest Publishers Inc.
450 Parkway Drive, Suite D
Broomall, PA 19008
www.masoncrest.com

Copyright © 2015 Mason Crest, an imprint of National Highlights Inc.

Library of Congress Cataloging-in-Publication Data on file at the Library of Congress and with the publisher

Series ISBN: 978-1-4222-3235-4
Hardback ISBN: 978-1-4222-3241-5
EBook ISBN: 978-1-4222-8670-8

First Edition: September 2005

Produced in association with Shoreline Publishing Group LLC

Printed and bound in the United States

IMPORTANT NOTICE

The techniques and information described in this publication are for use in dire circumstances only where the safety of the individual is at risk. Accordingly, the publisher copyright owner cannot accept any responsibility for any prosecution or proceedings brought or instituted against any person or body as a result of the use or misuse of the techniques and information within.

Picture Credits
Paul Clifton: 43, 57, 82.
Dollar Photo Club: WavebreakMicroMedia: 55; Avesun: 56.
Dreamstimes.com: Cyberlot: 22; Tobyimages: 17; Londonsip 30; Pojoslaw: 50.
Mary Evans: 15, 37.
Nathan Johnson: 6, 10, 13, 54, 61, 67, 84.
The Picture Desk / Kobal: 58.
Sporting Pictures: 8, 23, 24, 32, 89.
Bob Willingham: 18, 21, 38, 42, 74, 76.

Front cover image: Stace Sanchez/Kickpics

Contents

Introduction 6

Eastern Training Methods 8

Warm-Up and Preparation 24

Energy Work 34

Conditioning Basics 50

Fitness Example: Karate 58

Preventing Injury 74

Mental Training 82

Glossary 90

Clothing and Equipment 92

Further Reading 94

Useful Web Sites/About the Author 95

Index 96

Words to Understand: These words with their easy-to-understand definitions will increase the reader's understanding of the text, while building vocabulary skills.

Sidebars: This boxed material within the main text allows readers to build knowledge, gain insights, explore possibilities, and broaden their perspectives by weaving together additional information to provide realistic and holistic perspectives.

Two martial artists demonstrate their skills. These perfectly timed, acrobatic moves look effortless, but they require the highest levels of strength, stamina, and flexibility.

INTRODUCTION

The journey of a thousand miles begins with a single step, and the journey of a martial artist begins with a single thought—the decision to learn and train. The Martial Arts involve mental and emotional development, not just physical training, and therefore you can start your journey by reading and studying books. At the very beginning, you must decide which Martial Art is right for you, and reading these books will give you a full perspective and open this world up to you. If you are already a martial artist, books can elevate your training to new levels by revealing techniques and aspects of history and pioneers that you might not have known about.

The Mastering the Martial Arts series will provide you with insights into the world of the most well-known martial arts along with several unique training categories. It will introduce you to the key pioneers of the martial arts and the leaders of the next generation. Martial Arts have been around for thousands of years in all of the cultures of the world. However, until recently, the techniques, philosophies, and training methods were considered valuable secretes and seldom revealed. With the globalization of the world, we now openly share the information and we are achieving new levels of knowledge and wisdom. I highly recommend these books to begin your journey or to discover new aspects of your own training.

Be well.
Adam James

 WORDS TO UNDERSTAND

chi/qi Cosmic energy believed by the Chinese to animate all matter; humans acquire chi from food and from the environment; in the soft/internal martial arts, chi is used as a weapon

dojo Training hall used for all Japanese martial arts

karate-ka A student of karate-do, the art of the empty hand

Eastern Training Methods

The phrase "East and West, never the twain shall meet," is true where health-and-fitness training are concerned. While this form of training in the West becomes ever more specialized, Eastern training can be described as "holistic."

The aim of any fitness program is to develop muscular strength, aerobic (heart-lung) fitness, and flexibility. The Western approach is to treat these three main components of fitness as separate, with dedicated activities for each: weight-training for strength; running, swimming, or aerobics for heart-lung fitness; and stretching or yoga for flexibility. Often, little or no attention is paid to the other components of fitness, such as balance, coordination, and speed unless you are practicing a sport. (Although drills do exist to develop these skills, they are usually reserved for professional athletes.) For the average Western exerciser, any of the extra skills he or she learns are picked up randomly, while doing the activity or sport itself.

The martial arts have a different approach to fitness. Although martial artists will perform strengthening exercises, such as push-ups and sit-ups,

The martial arts provide an integrated training program suitable for students of any age. These young taekwondo martial artists are practicing their skills in a high-kicking drill.

and stamina-building exercises, such as running, these exercises occupy a comparatively small part of their overall training, the bulk of which is in the techniques of their chosen arts. Martial artists develop their strength and fitness by regularly practicing the techniques of their chosen arts. Indeed, one only has to think of a martial artist such as Bruce Lee to see how strong and fit a dedicated practitioner can become.

Training in the martial arts is also different from Western training

The process of learning never stops in the martial arts, as the difficulty of the techniques increases as your skills develop. This picture shows two karate black belts sparring.

WARNING

Although all the fitness techniques shown in this book are safe for a person of average fitness who has properly warmed up (see pp. 25–33), any exercise is potentially hazardous for a beginner, who may not be aware of how far to push him- or herself. You should always consult your doctor before beginning a new type of exercise. He or she will no doubt encourage you, but may have special advice for you if you suffer from high or low blood pressure, diabetes, or if you are pregnant. Should you feel any dizziness, acute pain, or excessive tiredness while performing any of the techniques or drills in this book, stop immediately and seek medical advice.

methods in that the complexity of the techniques learned increases as the training progresses. Unlike weight training or running—in which once you have learned the basics, you continue with the same techniques (with a few variations) for the rest of your training career—the martial arts always have something new to offer. Even for the most dedicated of practitioners, a single lifetime is not enough to learn all the styles and skills that the martial arts can teach.

GENERAL TRAINING GUIDELINES

One of the things that people find appealing about the martial arts is that the practice requires little or no equipment. You do not even have to go to an athletic club or gym. While you certainly can find excellent venues that provide formal training in the martial arts, it is not an absolute for someone wishing to study the martial arts.

When training, let common sense be your guide. For example, if you want to train outdoors, choose firm land that is sheltered from the wind. Training is best done in the morning, when the body and mind are rested, but you should train at the time that works best for you. Avoid training on a full stomach, as this can lead to problems. However, a light meal or snack before training is fine.

The Chinese do not encourage the display of the human body, in part for moral reasons, and also because of health concerns. When training, you should wear loose-fitting clothing, such as a t-shirt, sweatshirt, or tracksuit. When training outdoors, wear clothing that is appropriate to the season, layering in cold weather so that you can remove and replace layers as your body warms up and cools down.

You can train either barefoot or wearing flat-soled cloth slippers that give the foot some basic protection while providing a firm footing. Avoid wearing training shoes with thick soles. They will prevent you from feeling the ground beneath your feet. Avoid running shoes as well, as these are designed for stability while jogging or running, and provide little or no lateral support.

As you proceed in your chosen art, your fitness will improve as a natural consequence of performing the techniques correctly. This not only includes strength, stamina, and flexibility, but also the other skills mentioned, such as balance, coordination, and agility. And there is one more thing that the Chinese call **qi,** or **chi.** According to this philosophy, chi is the force that animates the cosmos; without chi, there would be no life. A full understanding of the martial arts is not possible without an appreciation of the concept of chi.

Agility, balance, coordination, and speed are all skills developed in the martial arts in addition to strength, stamina, and flexibility. A kung fu artist practices in solitude in an ornamental garden to settle his thoughts.

A BRIEF HISTORY OF THE MARTIAL ARTS

The martial arts of China, Korea, and Japan all have strong links with the religious faith of Buddhism. Why the world's most formidable fighting arts are linked to a religion that preaches respect for all life, as well as pacifism, is of more than passing historical interest.

Buddhism originated in northern India in the 6th century B.C. The historical Buddha, Prince Gautama Siddharta (563–483 B.C.), famously left his luxurious palace and family, opting for a life of hardship, and pledging not to rest until he had found enlightenment. After seven years, his search was rewarded and he became the Buddha, the Enlightened Being. His teaching is summarized in the Four Noble Truths: life is suffering; the root of suffering is illusion; illusion can be overcome and suffering ended; the way to overcome suffering is by following the Buddha's Eightfold Path (right thought, right action, right effort, right speech, right livelihood, right attention, right concentration, and right understanding). Although the Buddha rejected the yoga of India's holy men as one of the roads to salvation, the practices of certain forms of Buddhism (such as Zen, with its many hours

CHI AND THE WEST

The idea of chi has already penetrated Western consciousness. Along with the martial arts, the West has welcomed such arts as feng shui, which is the art of harnessing the chi found in the cosmos, and Traditional Chinese Medicine (TCM), which employs techniques such as acupuncture and herbalism to balance the chi that exists in the body.

The yin-yang diagram surrounded by the eight trigrams represents the Chinese Daoist view of the cosmos, which has had a profound impact on the development of the Chinese martial arts.

of meditation) is similarly physically demanding. Buddhism first came to China in the first century A.D. As the centuries passed, however, some of the Chinese Buddhist monks became lax with regards to practicing their faith, and Buddhism was tainted with ideas from China's other religion, Daoism (also known as Taoism) (see pp. 86–87). An Indian monk and religious reformer named Bodhidharma (known as Tamo in China) left for China in the year A.D. 517 to preach Dhyana, a form of Buddhism based on meditation. Arriving three years later, Bodhidharma was initially welcomed at the imperial court and was granted an audience with Emperor Wu. The emperor, however, was unable to understand Bodhidharma's teachings.

Bodhidharma retired to the Shaolin monastery at the foot of Songshan Mountain in Honan province. There, he found the monks to be holy and strong in spirit, but weak in body. He taught them a series of 18 exercises to enable them to meditate for longer periods of time.

Over the centuries, these exercises were expanded and then formalized into the Shaolin lohan boxing method. (A rather colorful version of Shaolin practices was presented by the 1970s cult-television series *Kung Fu*, starring David Carradine.) The monks' reputation grew, and eventually lay pupils came to the monastery to learn Shaolin lohan. Some of these pupils eventually set up their own Shaolin lohan schools. In time, a second Shaolin temple was established in the province of Fukien in Southern China. The monks of this temple created a second style of Shaolin kung fu, which became known as the "Southern school."

The Shaolin monks participated in Chinese politics and helped the Ch'ing Dynasty (1644–1911) take control of the country. Emperor K'ang Hsi eventually became suspicious of the monks, however, fearing that they would turn against him. In 1674, he ordered that the monasteries be stormed and burned to the ground and the monks and nuns slaughtered. Only five monks and nuns escaped the massacre; they are credited as the founders of the Shaolin martial arts styles in existence today.

While the Japanese and Koreans remained politically independent from China, they adopted both its form of imperial government and its Buddhist religion. They also imported the Chinese fighting arts. These arts were combined with native fighting techniques, and in time, they developed into distinct local styles: taekwondo in Korea, and karate and jujutsu in Japan.

China's martial arts are said to have been founded by an Indian Buddhist monk, Bodhidharma, who came to China and taught at the Shaolin monastery in Honan Province in the 6th century A.D. Statues of Buddhas are found throughout Asia, such as this one in India.

There is now a bewildering range of martial arts to choose from, from the traditional Chinese and Japanese arts, to newcomers, such as Brazil's acrobatic capoeira, shown here.

Today, there are hundreds of martial arts styles in existence in the world. It seems that every year, new styles—capoiera from Brazil, pentjak-silat from Indonesia, and Thai kickboxing, to name but three recent arrivals—are added to established arts such as wing chun, judo ("the way of suppleness"), and karate. All of these arts offer a complete and self-contained health, fitness, and fighting method, each of which often claims to be the best in the world. This leaves the prospective student with a dizzying array of choices: armed and unarmed styles, "hard" and "soft" styles, and attack and defensive arts, not to mention different teaching styles and environments.

WHICH MARTIAL ART?

Long gone are the days when prospective martial arts students had to spend days and nights kneeling outside the temple doors in the snow before they were considered worthy of admission, or when the secrets of an art might die with a master if he did not find a student worthy of his teaching. Today, classes are available at gyms and at martial arts **dojos.** Instead of the secrecy that used to surround the martial arts, today, there seems to be a rush to disseminate their teachings to as wide an audience as possible.

Finding a martial arts teacher that is right for you can take some time. The teaching styles of the Chinese, Koreans, and Japanese are all quite different and will suit different temperaments. The Koreans and Japanese have the most formalized training methods in the martial arts; most readers will have seen the ranks of white-clad **karate-ka**

WING CHUN

One of the best-known Chinese martial arts is wing chun. A martial artist named Yip Man taught wing chun in the West after leaving China after the Communist revolution and settling in Hong Kong. Man's aim was to make wing chun the world's most popular martial art. His most famous pupil, the actor and martial artist Bruce Lee, helped him spread its popularity.

(those who practice karate) striding, punching, and kicking in unison to the clipped military commands of their teacher.

The Japanese were the first to turn their once little-known and deadly fighting arts into national sports. The first judo school opened in Tokyo in 1882, and Shotokan karate was recognized as a sport in the first decades of the 20th century. Because of their long history as sports, judo and karate schools follow set curricula. There are regular exams, in which standards of proficiency are awarded and confirmed by the right to wear a colored belt. Beginners start with a white belt, progressing through the ranks to the right to wear different colored belts, until they reach the rank at which they can wear the coveted black belt. The black belt is not the highest qualification, however; a student can still take further exams, or dans (levels). The most senior practitioners sometimes revert to the white belt in order to symbolize the fact that even at the most advanced level, they have only just begun training.

Terminology, clothing, and dojo etiquette are standardized worldwide. This pattern, set by judo and karate, has been adopted by later Japanese martial arts, such as aikido ("the way of harmony"), and by the Korean martial arts, which have been influenced by the Japanese models.

The situation with the Chinese martial arts, however, is quite different. The chaotic state of China after the fall of the Ch'ing Dynasty in 1911 meant that there was no interest from the state in preserving China's fighting arts or in developing them into sports. On the contrary, many schools allied themselves with rival warlords and secret societies, known infamously as the Triads, and played an active role in China's protracted internal struggles.

When the Communist government took control of the country in 1949, it viewed China's traditional cultural heritage as an undesirable remnant of its hated imperial past. Many martial arts masters went into hiding or left the country, seeking refuge in non-communist Taiwan or the then-British colony of Hong Kong. It is only in recent decades that the Chinese government has looked more favorably upon the martial arts. In the 1970s, it recognized the martial art t'ai chi ch'uan ("great ultimate fist"), and promoted it as a form of health and fitness training.

Chinese methods of teaching are less formal than those of the Japanese or the Koreans. In the Chinese method, the individual teacher decides the curriculum. There are no examinations, nor is there a system of ranking by belts. A student's worth is measured by his or her ability to win bouts against his or her fellow students or against the students of rival schools.

A wing chun practitioner poses with sword. In Japan, the martial arts became sports in the early 20th century, but in China, martial artists used their fighting skills in politics well into the modern period.

Martial arts classes in the West reflect the teaching patterns of the particular martial art's country of origin. For example, Japanese arts are taught in the dojo, as is the Japanese way. Students are expected to wear a special martial arts suit, called a gi, and to learn the Japanese terminology for techniques. This approach suits students who prefer highly structured and disciplined environments.

Those with a more individualistic temperament might prefer the less-formal Chinese approach, but there are considerations here as well.

T'ai chi is a part of many people's workout routine, helping with balance.

Whereas an aikido, karate, or judo black belt is a recognized international qualification, the ability and qualifications of a self-styled Chinese martial arts master cannot be evaluated. Many Western students of the martial arts returned from East Asia in the 1980s and 1990s to found schools in Europe and the U.S., with no proof of their credentials apart from their claims to have been taught by a certain Chinese master.

The martial arts offer complete athletic conditioning systems, providing training in all of the major aspects of fitness, but they can also be used as

Japanese training methods, clothing, and gradings in aikido, judo, and karate are standardized worldwide, so that a black belt is a universally recognized qualification.

complementary forms of exercise to improve performance of other sporting activities. Indeed, professional athletes have long recognized the value of the mental training offered by the martial arts (see pp. 83–89). Many endurance athletes practice t'ai chi ch'uan (known in the West as t'ai chi), the slow movements of which promote relaxation and concentration. In addition to t'ai chi, the arts that might attract those interested in the spiritual side of the martial arts include kendo (Japanese fencing), iaido ("the way of the sword"), and kyudo (Japanese archery).

WORDS TO UNDERSTAND

ballistic Having to do with sudden, sharp movement

dynamic The characteristic of sudden change

Warm-Up and Preparation

First thing in the morning, your body is like a car that has been idle overnight. The engine is cold, the oil viscous and stagnant, the battery drained of power. Moreover, if you have an older model, you cannot expect to turn the key in the ignition and drive straight off without some waiting and coaxing.

The need for a thorough warm-up before any form of exercise, no matter how gentle it may appear, cannot be overstated. A great many sports injuries can be avoided with just a few minutes of warming up. The frequent kicks and rapid changes of direction that are found in many martial arts are demanding on the joints, so particular attention should be accorded to these areas.

There is no one way of warming up, but the general rule is to move and loosen up all the major joints and muscle groups of the body. The main joints are the wrists, elbows, shoulders, ankles, knees, hips, and the spine. The major muscle groups are the hamstrings and quadriceps, the large bundles of muscles at the front and rear of the thighs (these

The martial arts make particular demands on the body's joints and musculature in fast-paced, dynamic movements. Without a proper warm-up, the martial artist runs the risk of serious injury.

muscles are particularly vulnerable to tears and sprains when not properly warmed up); the two muscles that make up the calves; the tendon that attaches your heel to your calf (called the Achilles tendon); and the muscles of the arms, shoulders, back, and chest.

SHORT WARM-UP PROGRAM

Once you have changed into appropriate clothing (see guidelines on p. 12), you are ready to warm up. Although the exercises are merely a preparation, to be effective, they should be carried out with as much care and concentration as all other techniques. There are many options for warm-up activities including brisk walking, light jogging, bike riding, or other cardio exercise machines if available, like a treadmill, rowing machine, elliptical machine, or stepper. Also, one can do light calisthenics like jumping jacks, lunges, etc. For the martial artist, it's effective to warm up by gently performing Katas or forms, as well as doing shadow boxing/shadow fighting.

STRETCHING

Stretching builds on the effects of the warm-up, and properly prepares the body for rigorous exercise. Proper stretching will prevent injuries and enhance peak performance. There are several key principles of anatomy and physiology that dramatically affect stretching. First all stretches are either **dynamic** or static—in other words the body is either moving (dynamic) or it is not moving (static). Prior to exercise, which involves movement, it's very important to move during stretching. Dynamic stretching will allow the body to move through the range of motion for the joints and prepare it for exercise. Another principle of stretching is that all stretches are either active or passive – in other words the person is either moving the body or there is an external force that pushes the body through the range of motion. Static passive stretches are excellent for after exercise and can enhance range of motion (ROM); however, they can weaken muscles if done prior to exercise and diminish athletic performance. Dynamic active stretches are ideal before exercise and will prepare the body for movement. There are many stretches to choose from and the following exercises should give you a good starting point.

HEAD ROLLING

Stand in a relaxed position with your feet shoulder-width apart, your hands hanging loosely by your sides, and your back and head erect. Drop your head to the left, and tilt it so that you are looking at your left shoulder. Slowly roll your head forward to the center and then around, until you are looking at your right shoulder. Reverse the direction back to

SHOULDER ROLLS

Shrug your shoulders as high as possible and roll them forward and then backward.

WAIST ROTATIONS

With your arms swinging freely, rotate the waist from side to side.

the left. Repeat at least five times in each direction, moving slowly and smoothly and deepening the movement with each roll.

SHOULDER ROLLS

Work your way down your body by doing shoulder rolls. Stand in a relaxed position with your feet shoulder-width apart, your arms hanging loosely by your sides, and your back and head erect. Shrug your shoulders as high and as far forward as they will go, bringing your shoulder blades up and together. Now roll your shoulders back as far as they will go, and then lower them, depressing your shoulder blades and spreading your shoulders wide. Circle around until you are back at the starting position. Repeat at least five times, slowly and smoothly, before reversing the direction for a further five rolls. Keep the arms relaxed throughout, and do not jerk them up as you roll your shoulders.

WAIST ROTATIONS

From there, move on to waist rotations. Stand in a relaxed position with your feet hip-width apart, your arms hanging loosely by your sides, and your back and head erect. Begin turning from the waist slowly and smoothly, letting your arms move freely.

Increase the momentum gradually, and let your arms slap into your body with each turn. Make sure you turn from the waist, and not from the shoulders. Everything below your waist should be still, and everything above it should move as a single unit. Complete at least 10 rotations in each direction.

KNEE CIRCLES

Knee circles are another important warm-up exercise. Stand with your legs and feet together. Bend your knees, and rest your hands on your thighs. Begin making small circles with your knees in one direction, gradually increasing the size of the circle over at least 10 circles. Repeat for at least 10 circles in the opposite direction.

Caution is advised when doing this exercise. Your knee and ankle joints can be damaged when pressure is applied against their planes of movement. The knee, for example, will be injured if too much pressure is applied from the side. The martial arts can be demanding on the knees, with their low stances, rapid changes of direction, and kicking techniques. Thus, care should be taken to warm and stretch the legs thoroughly.

ARM AND LEG SWINGS

Move the arms and legs slowly though the range of motion. For example, bring your arm forward as far as you can and then move it back as far back behind you. Do not swing the arms or legs with excessive force,

The yoga pose known as "downward dog" can be the start of a "walking lunge." Move the hands forward while keeping the legs straight until you reach a pushup position. Then "walk" your hands backward to continue the stretch.

which can lead to injury. When momentum is used during the dynamic stretch, the movement becomes passive (no longer active). This makes the stretch **ballistic** and it will place excessive force on the joints. Be sure to avoid ballistic stretches and any bouncing during stretches.

SQUATS AND LUNGES

Another very effective stretch or range of motion exercise is the squat. Simply squat down as low as possible and return to the starting position. Walking lunges will also allow the body to go through a full range of motion and prepare the person for dynamic exercise.

BASIC STRETCHING

To improve range of motion, it is valuable to do static passive stretches after exercise. There are many different stretches but the following exercises give you a good starting point.

HAMSTRING STRETCH

To perform the hamstring stretch, stand with your feet apart. Take a step forward with your right leg. Keeping both legs straight and both feet flat on the ground, bend forward from the waist, as if you were trying to touch your knees with your chin. Put both hands on your leading leg for stability. Hold for five breaths, pushing a little further each time you exhale. Repeat for another five breaths with the left leg leading. This

SOME BENEFITS OF WARMING UP

Many people might think that a five-minute warm-up on a treadmill or a stationary bicycle is sufficient. While this will get the pulse rate up, the blood pumping, and the leg muscles and joints warm, it does not really warm up the spine or the upper-body joints and muscles. A good warm-up will give you the following important benefits:

Increases blood supply to the muscles

Limbers joints

Raises pulse rate

Mental preparation

Mobilizes chi

Protection from injuries

ANCIENT MARTIAL ARTS AND WEIGHTLIFTING

While many people think that weight lifting only recently became a part of martial arts athletic conditioning, it has been a part of karate and kung fu for hundreds of years. In China, the Shaolin temple used numerous training methods to develop their kung fu skills including lifting stones and rocks. Meanwhile, in Okinawa, the birthplace of karate, martial artists lifted weights with handles similar to modern kettle bells. It was also common for the Okinawan karate practitioner to wear iron getta (the traditional Japanese shoe) and practice their kicks. kung fu and karate athletes would hold the weights and practice their blocks, punches, even kicks.

is also known as a runner's stretch. In addition to standing, it's very effective to perform the hamstring stretch while sitting on the ground. Simply sit down and spread the legs as wide as possible. While keeping your back straight, reach out to each leg and to the middle between the legs. Also, you can lie on your back and bring your leg straight up. This can be very important for people who have back pain, as this will allow the hamstring to stretch while not endangering the lower back.

QUADRICEPS STRETCH

You may want to use a chair or a wall for support during this exercise. Stand with your legs together. Bend your right knee, and grab your right ankle with your right hand. Keeping your knees together, pull your right leg behind you and as high up as it will go. Hold for five beats, pulling a little higher each time. Repeat with the left leg.

CALVES STRETCH

For this exercise, which stretches the calves, you may again want a chair or a wall for support. Stand with your legs together, and then take a long step forward (like a lunge). Keeping your head and back erect, your rear knee straight, and your back foot flat on the ground, push forward from your hips. You should feel a strong stretch in your lower leg. Hold for five beats, pushing a little further each time. Repeat with the other leg. When doing this exercise, do not let your leading (bent) knee go over and beyond your toes, as this can put strain on the joint. Your knee should be bent directly over your toes, forming a right angle.

BICEP STRETCH

Stand in a relaxed position with your feet apart. Keeping your head and back erect and your arms straight, flex your wrists so that your palms are facing the floor, with your fingers pointing forward. Slowly push your arms straight back without bending your elbows. Hold for five breaths, pushing a little further back each time.

SPINE STRETCH

To stretch the spine, kneel on all fours, with your hands under your shoulders and knees bent at a 90-degree angle. Take a deep breath, drop your head, and arch your spine as much as you can. Breathe out, and hollow your spine as much as possible while raising your head and tilting it back. Repeat five times.

 WORDS TO UNDERSTAND

chi gung (Chinese: energy work; also qi gung); techniques designed to increase and control the chi in the body to improve health and fitness

Energy Work

The Chinese believe that one of the intangible benefits of training in the martial arts can be found in the concept of chi (or qi). Chi is defined as the force that animates the cosmos, without which there would be no movement or life.

According to the ancient Chinese, chi is found in the environment all around us and also within our own bodies. It drives the blood through our arteries and provides the spark that gives life to our muscles and brains. We take in chi whenever we eat and breathe, and we can also pick it up from the cosmos itself (if we are correctly attuned to it). Imbalances in bodily chi can make us ill and must be adjusted by taking herbs or by inserting needles into invisible channels known as the meridians (chi flows through the body along the meridians according to the teachings of the art of acupuncture).

If chi is freely available, the ancient Chinese reasoned, then it might be possible to increase its store in the body and thereby improve health and prolong life. Over two-and-a-half millennia, Chinese doctors

Martial artists increase and control chi (qi) by using a combination of physical posture, breathing, movement, and the power of the mind, both to improve their own fitness and to use in combat against others.

refined a series of techniques to manipulate chi that included diet, medical treatments, and physical exercises, which were known as **chi gung.**

It stands to reason that if chi can be used beneficially to heal, it could also be used to injure. The fighting arts that use chi in this way are called "soft," or "internal," arts, to differentiate them from the "hard," or "external," arts that rely on the strength and hitting power of bone and muscle.

Of all the internal arts, t'ai chi is the one best-known in the West, where it is often taught as a relaxation and health-promoting exercise. T'ai chi is, however, actually an awesome martial killing art. Unlike Shaolin lohan and many other Chinese martial arts, t'ai chi is not connected with Buddhism, but with China's other great religion, Daoism (also known as Taoism). One of the legends about it origins relates that a 13th-century Daoist monk, Chang San Feng, learned its techniques from a god in a dream.

One of Chang's disciples was Chen Chia Kou. Chen's family continued to teach and develop the art over the centuries, splitting it into several styles. In the 19th century, a Chen-family master was engaged by a druggist to teach the druggist's sons. One of the family's servants, Yang Lu Chan, watched the lessons in the family home's garden through a gap in the fence and later practiced the techniques in secret. Yang was so gifted that he was eventually accepted as a student in his own right. When he had become accomplished in the art, Yang went to Beijing, where he proved the effectiveness of t'ai chi as a fighting art by defeating all of the contenders in a kung fu tournament. He was even hired to train the Imperial Guard. Yang established a style of t'ai chi that is now among the most practiced throughout the world.

The basic t'ai chi techniques are contained in "the form," a set sequence of exercises that are typically performed in slow motion. Each style of t'ai chi has its own version of "the form"; these versions vary in length, from 24 movements to over 100.

The Chinese government created the Simplified Beijing Form, taking elements from several of the existing t'ai chi forms. This composite form is now practiced as a health and fitness exercise routine by millions all over China.

The two other arts usually classed along with t'ai chi as internal are hsing-i, which uses circular motions based on the eight trigrams of the I-Ching (Book of Changes), and pa-kua, which has the reputation of being one of the most difficult of the internal arts. Unlike the circular motions of t'ai chi and hsing-i, pa-kua is linear. T'ai chi also teaches armed fighting technique forms involving the sword and the spear.

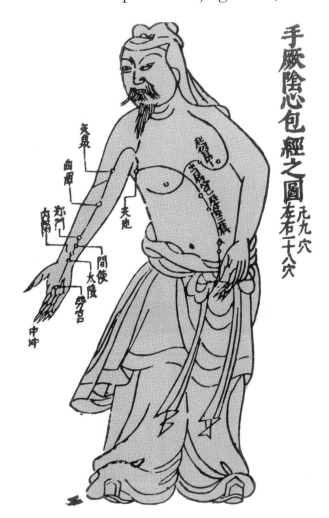

Chi (qi) flows through the body along invisible pathways, known as meridians, which are used by Chinese physicians in acupuncture treatments.

The postures and movements of the t'ai chi ch'uan form were modeled on the movements of real and mythical animals, such as the monkey and dragon.

The t'ai chi form can be categorized as chi gung (a technique for manipulating chi), since one of its main functions is to increase the amount of chi at the practitioner's disposal. T'ai chi also seeks to enable its practitioners to deliberately move chi in and out of their bodies.

The t'ai chi form is a complex subject that is beyond the scope of this book, but we will look at the "raising chi" exercise, which begins the form, followed by a series of chi gung exercises.

RAISING CHI

Stand with your feet parallel and hip-width apart. Your knees should be soft and your head and back straight, but your shoulders should be relaxed and your chest should be slightly sunken (rather than puffed out).

The ideal t'ai chi stance is that of an infant in his or her first years of walking, before stress and bad posture begin to affect the way he or she walks and stands. Your head should be balanced on top of your spine, without falling forward and rounding your upper back; your stomach muscles should be firm, but not clenched, and you should not be holding your stomach in; and your lower back should be naturally curved, but not hyperextended (so that your buttocks stick out). Your arms should hang freely at your sides. The fingers and thumbs of your hands should be aligned and touching, but relaxed. They should not be held straight, as in a "karate chop" hand.

Once you are settled into this posture, focus your attention on a point two inches (5 cm) below your navel. The Chinese call this point the dantian, and believe it is one of the main energy reservoirs in the body. Chi stored in the dantian, it is believed, can be redirected at will to other parts of the body. Keeping your focus in the dantian, begin to deepen and even out your breathing, so that your inhalations and exhalations are of the same length. Breathe more deeply than usual, but do not strain or force the air in or out by using your stomach muscles.

Once you have counted 10 slow-breathing cycles, breathe in and rotate your arms from the shoulder so that your palms face behind you. Your fingers and thumb should be aligned, but still relaxed. Breathe out, rotate your shoulders back to their starting position, and allow your hands to return

RAISING CHI

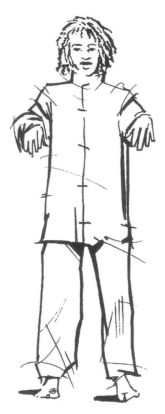

STEP 1: Stand with your feet shoulder-width apart, arms by your sides, fingers together, palms facing backward, knees soft.

STEP 2: Bend your knees and breathe in as you raise your hands slowly to chest height. The elbows remain relaxed and slightly bent.

to their natural hanging position. On the next inhalation, rotate your arms and palms again, raise your hands a couple of inches in front of you, and then lower them. Continue raising your hands a little further each time you inhale, until they reach chest level.

Your arms and hands should be completely relaxed, with your shoulder, elbow, and wrist joints fully open to allow the free flow of chi. Any stiffness or tension in your arms will block or impede the flow of chi. Your hands should be able to float up and down smoothly and slowly, as if they

STEP 3: Breathe in; imagine the chi entering your body and sinking into your dantian. Breathe out and lower the hands smoothly.

STEP 4: As your arms reach the starting position, straighten your legs. Repeat 10 times, drawing the chi into your dantian with your mind.

were in water.

Once you are comfortable with this exercise, breath in and out as you raise and lower your arms, and return your focus to the dantian. Imagine that the chi is entering your body with each breath. While the air goes into your lungs, the heavier chi sinks into your dantian, where it accumulates one drop at a time. Each time you exhale, feel all the toxins and poisons leaving your body. Continue this exercise until you have done 10 or more full movements (with the hands up to shoulder height). You may experience a warming

Once students have mastered the basic t'ai chi ch'uan form, they continue their training with the much faster-paced sword and spear forms.

of your body and some tingling in your hands as you perform this exercise, both of which are a natural effect of it.

CHI GUNG

There are literally thousands of chi gung techniques, some with medical uses, others specifically designed for training in the martial arts. Regardless of whether the style they practice is hard/external or soft/internal, Chinese martial artists all include chi gung exercises in their training programs. While performing the chi gung exercises shown on pp. 44–49, keep your focus on your breath and on the chi entering your dantian, just as in the

raising chi exercise on the previous pages. Perform each exercise from three to six times, moving through the sequences slowly and smoothly. In addition to increasing and balancing the chi flowing in your body, these exercises each have specific health benefits, as they stimulate the different meridians. From the point of view of athletic conditioning, they will also assist you in improving your coordination, balance, and posture. Perform them after your warm-up routine and before any more strenuous training in stances or drills.

OPENING THE CHEST

STEP 1: Stand in shoulder-width stance, arms easy by your sides, head back and straight, and bend your knees. Breathe in. Raise your arms to chest height, and position your hands so that your palms face one another. Breathe out.

STEP 2: Breathe in, separate your arms to open your chest, and straighten your knees.

STEP 3: Continue opening your arms, expanding your chest fully.

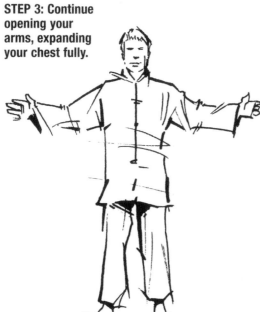

STEP 4: Breathe out, and bend your knees. Bring your arms to the center of your body, and then lower them to the starting position.

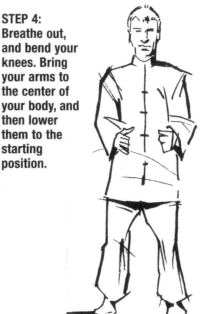

SEPARATING THE CLOUDS

STEP 1: Stand with your feet shoulder-width apart, your arms by your sides. Breathing out, cross your arms in front of you, left hand over right, as you bend your knees.

STEP 2: Breathe in as you raise your arms over your head, straightening your knees.

STEP 3: Separate your hands as they rise above your head.

STEP 4: Press directly upward with your palms facing the sky.

STEP 5: Breathe out, and lower your hands.

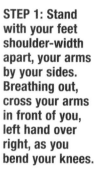

PUSHING PALMS WHILE TURNING WAIST

STEP 1: Stand with your feet shoulder-width apart, with your hands by your sides, palms up. Breathe out. Draw back your right hand, turn your waist to the left, and push your right palm forwards.

STEP 2: Breathe in. Draw your right hand back. As you move, turn your waist back to the center. Cross your palms in front of you.

STEP 3: Begin to shift your weight to your right foot and to draw back the right hand as you breathe out.

STEP 4: As you exhale fully, push forward with the left palm. Continue moving through the sequence slowly and smoothly.

CLOUD HANDS

STEP 1: Stand with your feet slightly wider than shoulder-width apart, your knees bent and your arms by your sides. Breathe out. Raise your left hand (with the palm facing you) up to face level, and bring your right hand (with the palm facing you) up to waist height.

STEP 2: Breathe in. Turn to the left from your waist. Lower your left hand, and raise your right hand, with your palm facing up.

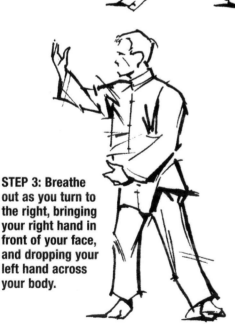

STEP 3: Breathe out as you turn to the right, bringing your right hand in front of your face, and dropping your left hand across your body.

STEP 4: In effect, you are making two linked circles in the air in front of you as you shift your weight from one foot to the other by turning at the waist.

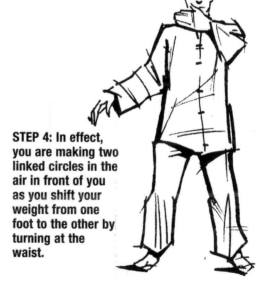

SCOOPING THE SEA WHILE LOOKING AT THE SKY

STEP 1: Stand with your feet shoulder-width apart, your knees soft, and your arms by your sides. Breathe out. Take a step forward with your left foot, and shift your weight onto it; your right knee is straight, with the foot on the floor. Stretch your arms out in front of you.

STEP 2: Lean forward, bringing your hands together ahead of your left knee. Bend your knee further, but do not allow it to go over the toes of your left foot.

STEP 3: Breathe in as you begin to shift your weight back from your left to your right foot. Open and draw back your arms.

STEP 4: Look up as you open your arms wide. Return to the starting position, and repeat the exercise with the right leg.

 WORDS TO UNDERSTAND

cardiovascular Having to do with the heart and its actions

Conditioning Basics

The key to training at a high level and staying injury free is balance. A martial artist must train with a proper understanding of all the different aspects of their chosen discipline and fitness in general. Modern exercise science reveals that there are several important factors, and an athlete must include all of them to achieve maximum results.

By Adam James

According to the National College of Exercise Professionals, here are the main components of fitness.

• Flexibility Training: A martial artist must be flexible to reach the extreme positions in kicks, but also must prevent injuries. Correct flexibility training includes using active-dynamic stretching to begin exercise and static-passive stretching at the end of a workout. It's important to always warm up properly before stretching and to not bounce while stretching. It's important to note that tendons and ligaments are not meant to stretch, and improper flexibility training can cause injuries to

The modern way to get ready for martial arts or any type of sport is with a warm-up routine that involves movement, stretching, and flexibility.

MARTIAL ARTS FOR ATHLETIC CONDITIONING

BEFORE YOU CARDIO

Before beginning strenuous cardiovascular training, it's wise to perform three tests: the Talk Test, the Leveling Test, and the Recovery Test. First, find the person's resting heart rate by taking their pulse. Next, calculate a training heart rate range by subtracting the person's age from the number 220 (this is their maximum heart rate). Then multiply by 50 percent to get the initial testing heart rate range.

To begin, the person should perform light activity (like walking or jogging on a treadmill) and get their heart rate into the training range. Once the heart rate is in the range of 50 percent of the maximum heart rate, maintain the level of intensity of the exercise (in other words, don't go any faster or harder on the treadmill, for example).

Start with the Talk Test: See if the person can talk comfortably while in the training heart rate range. Next, perform the Leveling Test: check if the person's heart rate has leveled off while the intensity of the exercise has leveled off (in other words, check if their heart rate is still going up even though the exercise hasn't increased in intensity). After 10-15 minutes in the heart rate range, the person stops the exercise and rests for 2-3 minutes. Now perform the Recovery Test: retake pulse and determine if their heart rate has returned to within 10-15 beats of their resting heart rate. A person who does not pass one or more of the three tests should see a physician before starting an exercise program.

the joints, both short term and long term. However, when performed correctly, stretching can prevent injuries to the athlete.

• **Cardiovascular** Training: also sometimes called simply cardio, this component of fitness is about conditioning the heart to pump blood more efficiently through the body. To be in top physical condition, the martial artist must train the heart muscle. However, you can't lift weights with your heart muscle. The cardiac muscle of the heart becomes stronger by elevating the heart rate and maintaining it for a period of time.

For proper cardiovascular training, the martial artist should perform rhythmic activity like jogging, biking, swimming, fast walking, or using a cardio machine such as an elliptical machine or a rowing machine. The person should monitor their heart rate and get it into the range of 50-85 percent of their maximum heart rate (which is 220 minus their age). For a person who is working out for the first time and not in top shape, they should train closer to the 50-70 range for 15-20 minutes two to three times per week. The highly conditioned athlete should get their heart rate in the 70-85 range for 20-30 minutes four to six times per week.

• Resistance Training: also know as weightlifting, this important aspect of fitness will enhance muscle endurance, strength, and power. The National College of Exercise Professionals advocates training with resistance with these goals in mind.

Create balance and stability by always using proper form when lifting weights. Work with a professional to make sure you know how to

There are many two-handed drills in the martial arts, such as push hands in t'ai chi ch'uan, in which the aim is to "read" the other person's energy.

do each lift safely and properly.

Build endurance by increasing how many times you do a lift, called repetitions or "reps." After you have the proper form down, perform the exercise for 12-20 reps and one to three sets with 20-30 seconds rest between sets. Building endurance is important to prevent injuries and to enable higher levels of intensity.

Build muscle over time by doing fewer reps at a slower pace.

Develop maximum strength by doing 80-100 percent of your maximum weight for one to five reps at a time. Do three to five such sets resting about three minutes between each.

Finally, build the explosive muscle power needed in martial arts by doing lifts with very little weight but with higher reps.

To get the most out of your lifting, all resistance training should be executed with proper form. Try to exercise standing up, not sitting down. Free weights and body weight exercises are preferable to seated machines, and always use proper breathing and core stability.

• Nutrition: While there are many different views on what a person should eat, it's important to establish basic nutrition goals. Your doctor can help you create the right diet for you, but the National College of Exercise Professionals suggests these cornerstones for healthy eating habits:

Eat four to six small meals throughout the day. This helps keep the body's metabolic rate up. However, be careful of eating too much at each meal. Good portion control is vital to getting results.

Avoid eating refined foods, especially sugar. Whole, natural foods contain more nutrients and they are better for an athlete's performance and recovery. Refined foods contain additives and preservatives, and

Natural food like fruit makes for better snacking, while providing sweetness to your diet in a way that avoids refined sugar.

The final step in preparing for any martial art is to ready the mind. Meditation, visualization, and similar exercises are as important as stretching muscles.

MENTAL FITNESS

The final component of fitness according to the National College of Exercise Professionals is Attitude Training, also known as Mental Training. For thousands of years, martial artists have practiced training the mind through meditation and empowerment statements (known today as affirmations). Meditation is an exercise that will clear the mind of distractions and focus the attention and will power. Affirmations are short, positive, and powerful statements that affect the subconscious mind. Examples include: "I feel good, I feel great, I feel terrific!", "To me, nothing is impossible", and "I have a super strong mind, a super strong body, and a super strong spirit!"

people should limit anything that comes in a can, box, or wrapper.

Watch fat intake. While fat is an important nutrient, too much fat and the wrong type are detrimental to good health. People benefit from eating foods that have unsaturated fat and should avoid trans fat. In particular, omega 3 is valuable and it is found in fish oil and flax seeds.

Proper supplements: The fitness industry is awash with unnecessary supplements, and most people have no need for them. However, almost everyone will benefit from taking a multivitamin.

 WORDS TO UNDERSTAND

kiai The shouting technique used to emphasize action in karate

FITNESS EXAMPLE: KARATE

Every martial art calls for overall physical and mental fitness. But once you've chosen a martial art to start learning, you'll find that each has its own practices. You'll want to find one that meets your fitness goals, as well as one that is within your abilities. Karate is probably the most popular "beginner" martial art. We'll use it as an example to show how martial arts can be part of a fitness routine.

Karate has its origins in the Ryukyu Islands, which are situated south of Japan (Okinawa is the largest island). The island chain sits between Japan and China, and has been the scene of both contact and conflict between the two great East Asian empires. The Japanese invaded the Ryukyu Islands in 1609. They immediately abolished the local military caste, and banned the carrying of weapons in order to snuff out the possibility of any armed resistance. What they had not counted on, however, was that the islanders had learned unarmed fighting techniques from their Chinese neighbors. The islanders put up stiff resistance, using an art that was then known as Okinawate

Bruce Lee's superb lean, muscular physique demonstrates how effective martial arts training can be to control body weight, while at the same time giving the body muscular strength and endurance.

("Okinawa hand"), and also by turning agricultural implements, such as the tonfa (the handle of a rice grinder) and the kama (a sickle), into makeshift weapons. The Japanese responded by forbidding the study and practice of the islands' native martial arts. The islanders, however, continued to study and develop Okinawate in secret.

Over the centuries, the islanders accepted Japanese rule, but it was not until the beginning of the 20th century that the Japanese authorities recognized the value of Okinawate as a sporting discipline. In 1912, a young schoolteacher named Funakoshi Gichin gave a demonstration of Okinawate to a visiting admiral of the Imperial Japanese Navy. The admiral was so impressed that a few years later, Funakoshi was invited to Tokyo to give a demonstration in front of the Emperor. Funakoshi went on to open the first karate dojo in mainland Japan, called the Shotokan. Okinawate was renamed karatedo ("the way of the empty hand"), and remains one of the most popular styles of karate in the world. Other teachers followed Funakoshi to Japan to

THE ART OF KARATE

Although Shotokan karate—one of the most popular styles of karate— makes use of ki (Japanese for chi) in the **kiai** (shouting technique), it is primarily a hard, external art, like the hard-style Chinese Shaolin lohan. Karate training develops great physical strength and stamina through intense training in kata and kumite (non-contact sparring). The karate-ka (one who practices karate) makes effective use of his or her natural weapons to deliver stunning blows against an opponent's most vulnerable spots.

The art of karate was quickly recognized as a highly efficient form of health and fitness training by the Japanese government in the 1920s. Training in non-contact kata is particularly effective for children and adults alike.

teach other styles of Okinawate, and several of Funakoshi's senior disciples went on to found their own karate schools and styles.

KATA

The following exercises are based on karate kata training, which develops both muscular strength and aerobic fitness. They build on the stances detailed in the previous section, so ensure that you are familiar with the four basic stances before beginning this section. It is also important to follow the warm-up guidelines before attempting any kata drills.

The basic components of the kata are punches, blocks, and kicks.

You should vary the height of the delivery of your punches and kicks; they can be high (jodan), to the face; middle (chudan), to the torso; or low (gedan), to the groin or abdomen.

When practicing the techniques, imagine that you are fighting an imaginary attacker, and target specific parts of his or her anatomy with your strikes.

Never practice with a live partner, as any mistakes could have serious consequences. Once you have learned the techniques, you might want to practice on a punching bag, but start soft and slow, as a mistimed or misdirected kick can lead to a broken toe.

PUNCHING TECHNIQUES

The basic punch with the fist has a role to play in all the world's major fighting systems. In fitness applications, training in punches will improve stamina, speed, coordination, and accuracy. In their martial arts applications, punches have been made more effective by adding hand rotations at the end of the strike and the involvement of the whole body in the punching action.

THE LUNGE PUNCH

To perform the lunge punch (junzuki), start in a front stance with your left foot leading, your right hand in a fist on your hip, and your left hand extended straight out in front of you, also making a fist. Bring your right foot forward so that it passes close to your left foot, which is turned out slightly. Your right foot continues forward, forming a forward stance. As you shift your weight onto your right foot, snap your left fist back to your hip and simultaneously punch with your right fist. Rotate

THE LUNGE PUNCH

STEP 1: Start in a front stance with your left foot leading and your left arm extended in a fist in front of you.

STEP 2: Step forward into a right front stance, and punch with your right fist while pulling back your left fist to your hip.

both fists at the end of the movement. Your hips should end facing forward squarely, with your feet hip-width apart and with 60 percent of your weight on the front foot.

THE REVERSE PUNCH

STEP 1: Start from a left front stance, but with the right fist extended and the left at your hip.

STEP 2: Step forward and simultaneously punch with your left fist and pull back with your right.

STEP 3: Finish in a right front stance, rotating both fists as you hit the imaginary target.

THE REVERSE PUNCH

For the reverse punch (gyakuzuki), stand in a left front stance (see pp. 52–53). Punch once, so that your hands are now in the correct position (your right hand at your hip and your left arm outstretched). Turn your left foot out, and slide your right foot past it. As you complete the step, draw back your leading fist and punch with the other one, rotating both as you strike. Your hips should end facing forward squarely, with your feet hip-width apart and with 60 percent of your weight on the front foot.

KICKING TECHNIQUES

Kicks are extremely powerful techniques, from the point of view of both fitness and self-defense. The leg muscles are the largest in the body, so movements that involve lifting the legs will develop strength and stamina, as well as flexibility in the hip joint. In self-defense applications, the legs power killer blows delivered with various parts of your feet.

THE FRONT KICK

The front kick (maegeri) begins in a modified front stance, with your left leg leading and your legs hip-width apart. For this kick, your weight should be evenly distributed on both feet (rather than 60 percent on one foot and 40 percent on the other, as in the regular front stance). Place your arms out in front of you in a defensive posture. Your left fist should be at chest height, with the elbow bent, and your right fist should be at stomach height. Bring your arms back, turn your left foot in slightly, shift your weight onto it, and lift your right foot off the ground. Do not lift the foot heel-first; lift it up evenly. Lift your knee as high as it will go (eventually,

FRONT KICK

STEP 1: Standing in front stance, lift the foot sole-down.

STEP 2: Once your knee is as high as it will go, extend the leg to strike.

you will want to reach your opponent's head), and extend your leg forward. Aim to strike the target with the large, fleshy pad just under your toes. Lower the leg into a right forward stance, with your arms in the same position as before, but with the right arm leading.

THE BACK KICK

For the back kick (ushirogeri), begin in a right rear stance (see pp. 52–53), facing your imaginary opponent. Turn to the right, and take a step back with your left leg, toes facing away from your opponent. Shift your weight onto your left foot. Now your back is facing your opponent. Lift your right foot and thrust it back in a straight line, heel-first, at your chosen target. Drop your legs.

THE SIDE KICK

The side kick (yokogeri) begins in horse stance (see pp. 52–53), with the weight equally on both

To perform your kicks and punches properly, always imagine that you are striking an opponent. Choose your target height, aiming for head, body, or legs.

feet. Lean to your left, shifting your weight onto your left foot, and raise your right knee. Twist slightly on your left leg as you thrust the side of your foot at your imaginary opponent.

THE ROUNDHOUSE KICK

For the roundhouse kick (mawashigeri), begin from a left modified front stance (see pp. 52–53), turn your shoulders to the left, and lift your right foot. With your hips following your shoulders, turn your supporting foot counterclockwise approximately 60 degrees. Bring your knee across the front of

MARTIAL ARTS FOR ATHLETIC CONDITIONING

BACK KICK

STEP 1: Stand in rear stance, facing your imaginary opponent. Turn to the right.

STEP 2: Shift the weight to the left foot, and kick straight back with the right heel.

SIDE KICK

STEP 1: Starting in horse stance, lean to the left and raise your right knee.

STEP 2: Extend the right leg to strike with the side of your foot.

ROUNDHOUSE KICK

STEP 1: Starting from a left front stance, turn to the left and raise your right foot.

STEP 2: Bring your foot across your body to strike with your instep.

your body as you continue rotating your hips. Strike your imaginary opponent with your instep (the top of your foot). Place your foot down into a new modified front stance.

DRILLS

Repetition through drilling is an important teaching method in the martial arts. The more times you repeat a movement, the deeper it is engrained in your "body memory," so that when the time comes to use a technique in a fighting situation, you will react automatically, without losing valuable time thinking through your actions.

The first drill begins in the horse stance. Standing in a low, wide stance, punch alternately with your fists, drawing the other hand back to the hip. Remember to rotate the fists. Perform 20 strikes with each fist.

FORWARD BEND

STEP 1: Sitting with your legs outstretched in front of you, bend forward from the hips and grab your legs or feet.

STEP 2: Keeping your feet together and your knees on the floor, try to touch your knees with your head.

In the next drill, you will practice punching techniques. In an open area, perform both punches (see pp. 62–65) while moving across the room. Do at least 20 punches (10 on each side). A third drill is to practice kicking techniques, doing at least 20 of the four described kicks (see pp. 65–69), standing in the appropriate stance. The rear, front, and roundhouse kicks should all be performed while moving.

COMBINATIONS

Once you are confident performing punches and kicks, both standing and in motion, you can begin to combine them with one another. Here are some of the most basic combinations: front kick followed by a reverse punch; front kick, roundhouse kick, then a reverse punch; roundhouse kick, back kick, then a reverse punch.

Practice these combinations until you are comfortable with them, and then create your own ones. Your combinations can also include blocking techniques if you wish.

CIRCUIT TRAINING

After a warm-up, a typical karate session begins with 10 minutes of circuit training, the class performing several sets of exercises in between runs around the dojo. If practicing in a small space, run in place or skip rope for three minutes between each exercise. Perform the following circuit three times.

PUSH-UPS

Begin the circuit with some push-ups. Drop into a push-up position, but support your body on your fists rather than on the palms of your hands. Your fists should be shoulder-width apart, and your body and legs should be rigid, not sagging. Do at least 10 push-ups, eventually working your way up to 30.

FORWARD BEND

Do a forward bend by sitting with your legs together and straight out in front of you, and bending forward from the waist. Grab hold of your toes if

PUSH-UPS

STEP 1: In the martial arts push-up, rest your body weight on your clenched fists and feet.

STEP 2: Raise and lower your body, making sure that the back remains flat.

THE BUTTERFLY

STEP 1: Sit with the palms of your feet together and your knees as low as possible.

STEP 2: Grab your feet with your hands, and bend forward from the waist.

you can, your legs if you cannot. Applying steady pressure rather than jerking, pull yourself forward for a count of 30 seconds.

LUNGES

Lunges are the next exercises in this circuit. Begin by standing with your feet together and your hands on your hips. Take a long step forward with your right leg, and bend your right knee at a 90-degree angle. Drop the left knee slightly, but do not let it touch the floor. Pull back and repeat with the left leg leading until you have performed 10 lunges on each side.

THE BUTTERFLY

The next exercise is called the butterfly. Sit on the floor, and draw the soles of your feet together, pulling them close to your body. Gently push your knees to the ground and hold for 30 seconds.

BOX SPLITS

Sit with your legs open as wide as they will go. Your feet should point upward. Keeping your legs flat on the floor, bend forward from the waist. Support your weight with your hands.

THE BOX SPLITS

The next exercise is called the box splits. Sit with your legs open as wide as you can. Put your hands in front of you and, without allowing your legs to rotate (the feet must not roll forward), walk yourself forward with your hands, trying to lie flat out on the ground. Go down as far as you can, and hold for 30 seconds.

For the next exercise, lie on your back and raise your bent legs into the air. Put your hands flat by your sides. Keeping your head and upper body on the floor, raise your hips straight up, about two inches (about 5 cm) off the floor. Repeat 10 times, building up to 30 repetitions.

The final exercise in the circuit is called the box side stretch. Sitting as in the box splits, turn to face your right leg, and bend forward from the waist, trying to touch your knee with your forehead. Hold for 30 seconds, and then perform on the left side.

 WORDS TO UNDERSTAND

tatami Woven straw mat used as flooring in traditional Japanese houses and dojos

Preventing Injury

Injury prevention is an extremely important aspect of athletic conditioning for the simple and obvious reason that when an injured person cannot train, his or her health and fitness suffers as a result.

Among the most common injuries in sports are falls. Even a minor fall can cause a sprained ankle; a broken leg, arm, or wrist; a dislocated shoulder; or, more seriously, a head injury. Naturally, the martial arts have developed techniques to protect practitioners from all types of injury. These include blocks against punches and kicks, and break-falls and rollouts against throws.

The techniques in this section are taken from the Japanese arts of judo and aikido ("the way of harmony"). Both of these arts, which are relatively recent creations, share the far older martial art of jujutsu ("the compliant art") as their common ancestor. Jujutsu is Japan's original martial art, and was used by both the samurai and ninja in unarmed combat. Influenced by Chinese martial art styles, it employs a blend of striking and throwing techniques, as well as joint locks and strangles. Kano Jigoro, the founder of judo, and Ueshiba Morihei, the founder of aikido, were both jujutsu masters before they went on to create their own unique styles.

These are sometimes called Japan's "soft" arts, but they are quite

Abrasion injuries from falls, stray strikes, and throws are common in full-contact martial arts, such as Thai kickboxing, shown here.

Martial artists have to guard against all kinds of injuries, from falls to contact injuries, from stray punches and kicks, as well as weapons. Here, an aikido-ka prepares to deal with an attacker armed with a staff.

different from China's "soft" arts, t'ai chi, hsing-i, and pa-kua. While the Chinese arts are based on striking techniques, judo and aikido use throws to deflect or neutralize an opponent's attack, and joint locks, hold-downs, and strangles to control the opponent. There are no kata in judo and aikido; students learn new techniques from the teacher and practice them during free-sparring sessions. Students progress through the rankings by taking regular grading exams, during which they demonstrate their mastery of progressively more difficult techniques. Practitioners develop high degrees of flexibility, balance, coordination, speed, and stamina.

Judo and aikido are defensive arts. The basic principle of these arts is to use the opponent's own strength against him or her. Size and brute strength, therefore, are not always advantages in judo, and definitely not in aikido. For example, it is an aikido cliché in Japan for the large hulking Western beginner to be paired with a much smaller, demure Japanese girl, who proceeds to thrash and throw him around the dojo.

BACKWARDS BREAK-FALL

STEP 1: Squat on the edge of a padded surface. Tuck your head and arms in.

STEP 2: Allow yourself to fall backwards, keeping your back rounded.

STEP 3: As your shoulders touch the floor, slap the ground with your hands and forearms.

SIDEWAYS BREAK-FALL

STEP 1: Starting low, break your own balance so you fall sideways.

STEP 2: Keep your head turned away from the direction of the fall.

STEP 3: Slap the floor with your palm and forearm as your shoulder touches the floor.

BREAK-FALLS

The way to succeed in break-falls is to start slow, small, and low, gradually increasing the height, range, and speed of the movement. Begin your practice on something soft: a layer of cushions or a mattress, for example. In judo and aikido dojos, the flexible wooden floor is covered in **tatami** mats (mats made of woven rice straw). These mats provide a firm surface, but are also yielding, like thick turf. You should practice break-falls in every direction in which you are likely to fall: forwards, backwards, and to both sides.

BACKWARDS BREAK-FALL

To do a backwards break-fall, squat at the edge of your padded training area, with your head tucked in and your arms crossed at chest height. Make sure your mouth and teeth are closed to avoid any biting injuries. Round your spine, and let yourself roll backwards until your shoulders are on the floor. As you feel your shoulders come into contact with the floor, slap the ground with your palms and forearms at a 45-degree angle to your body; this action will stop your backward momentum and absorb the impact. Once you are at ease with this technique, try it out on a carpet. Begin to gradually increase the height from which you fall until you are standing upright and can fall backwards without hitting your head. With time and repeated practice, you will find that your body will become familiar with the action.

SIDEWAYS BREAK-FALL

For the sideways break-fall, tuck your head into the shoulder that is opposite to the direction of the fall. For example, if you are falling to the right, tuck your head to the left. Cross your leg to break your own balance, and allow yourself to fall to the side. Slap the mattress or floor with your palm and forearm; this action will ensure that your arm (rather than your body) absorbs the energy of the fall. As with the backwards break-fall, the timing of the slap is crucial: it should come just as your shoulder hits the floor. Slap too early, and you may injure your arm; slap too late, and you may injure your shoulder. As with the backwards break-fall, start in a low squatting position on a padded surface before attempting the standing version.

FORWARDS BREAK-FALL

For the forwards break-fall, begin in a low crouching position on a padded surface. Then dive forward onto your palms and forearms, allowing your elbows to give under your weight.

THE ROLLOUT

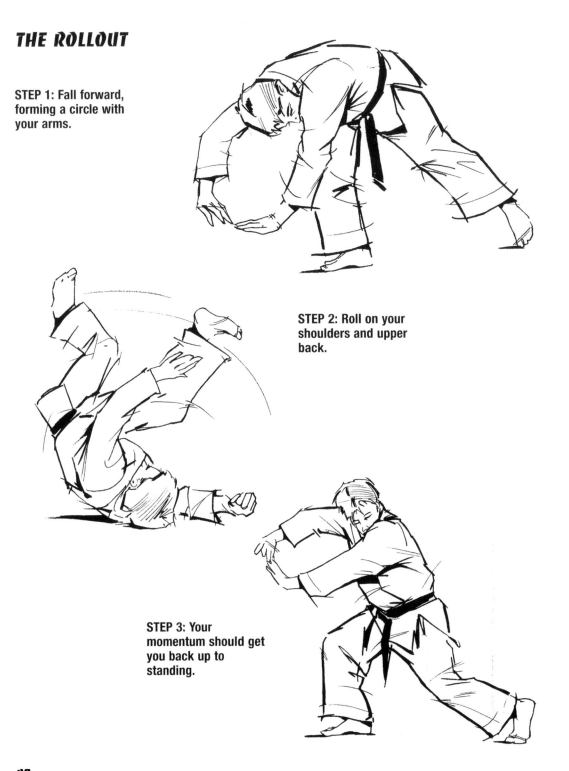

STEP 1: Fall forward, forming a circle with your arms.

STEP 2: Roll on your shoulders and upper back.

STEP 3: Your momentum should get you back up to standing.

ROLLOUT

An alternative to the forwards break-fall is the aikido rollout, which is more dynamic. When falling forward, reach out and form a circle with your arms. Tuck your head in, roll over your arms and back, and return to the standing position.

DRILLS

Beginners in judo, aikido, and jujutsu are repeatedly drilled in break-falls and rollouts until they are completely comfortable with them and they become an automatic response. During free sparring, there is no time to think, "I am being thrown. I need to perform a break-fall or rollout." In a surprise attack, there is even less time, if any, to think ahead and plan a response.

To perform a sideways break-fall drill, move across the length of a room or a training area outdoors using sideways break-falls, alternating between the right and the left. Perform at least 10 break-falls in each direction. To perform a rollout drill, move across the same distance using the aikido rollout.

Another type of drill, called the "up-and-over drill," is not for the fainthearted. In a dojo, a student is instructed to kneel and double over, protecting his or her head with his or her arms. The other students then run up and jump over the kneeling student, break-falling on the far side. After each jump, another student joins the student on the floor, doubling the length of jump for the next student. This continues until the class has run out of students—or until none of them will dare to jump over the line of bodies.

 WORDS TO UNDERSTAND

satori (Japanese: awakening); enlightenment desired by students of Zen Buddhism; this can be a sudden event, or one achieved after many years of meditation

seiza (Japanese: correct sitting); kneeling pose used in Japan for meditation as well as formal occasions

walking meditation Short period of walking during a Zen meditation to loosen the limbs after sitting meditation (or zazen)

zendo Meditation hall in a Japanese Zen monastery or temple

MENTAL TRAINING

Mental or spiritual training is a major aspect of all the martial arts. The martial arts' "spirit" is synonymous with self-discipline, concentration, and control. Training in the martial arts has other benefits as well, including the alleviation of stress-related problems and the improvement of athletic performance. Professional athletes from fields as varied as boxing and baseball employ relaxation, breathing, visualization, and meditation techniques borrowed from the martial arts.

The techniques for mental and spiritual training followed by martial artists schooled in East Asian methods come from two great religious traditions: Buddhism and Daoism. We have already seen the link between Buddhism and the Chinese martial arts with the emergence of the Shaolin fighting tradition (see p. 16), but in Japan, it was Zen Buddhism that had the greatest impact on the martial arts.

Zen is an austere form of Buddhism that teaches that we can attain enlightenment (**satori**) during our lifetime. There are two main traditions of Zen, each with a slightly different approach. The Soto

The mental and spiritual dimensions of training are at the center of martial arts training, in the development of what has become known as the "spirit of the martial arts."

The martial arts' close links with Buddhism means that many martial artists make use of Buddhist meditation techniques to aid their concentration.

school holds that enlightenment is reached gradually, over years of meditation, while the Rinzai school believes that enlightenment is a violent insight that can suddenly overtake a person at any time or place, regardless of training. In addition to zazen meditation (sitting meditation in which the student's only focus is his or her own breathing), the Zen Roshi (master) will give his students riddles or stories (called koan) to solve. One of the most famous is, "What is the sound of one hand clapping?" Zen first reached Japan in the seventh century, but it only became widespread from the 12th century on, with the rise of the samurai class. With its austerity, stress on self-discipline, and resignation in the face of hardship, Zen Buddhism appealed to the samurai warriors who ruled Japan from the 12th to 19th centuries. Today, it has particularly close links to the arts of kendo, iaido, and kyudo (Japanese archery)—arts whose use in fighting have long been superseded by firearms and are now largely spiritual pursuits.

Zazen meditation is performed in a Zen meditation hall (called a **zendo.**) It is usually performed for two-hour sessions in 40-50 minute periods, with a 10-minute interval of **walking meditation**. The zendo is an austere place without decorations that might distract the student. Japanese discipline is harsh, and any student seen to be falling asleep during meditation is struck on the shoulder with a bamboo cane.

ZAZEN MEDITATION

To practice zazen meditation, sit cross-legged or kneel in **seiza** (formal kneeling position), sitting on your heels. This position might be difficult at first. If you feel any discomfort, kneel on a large, flat cushion, and place a smaller one under your buttocks to raise them, thereby releasing the pressure on your ankles and knees.

You can also practice zazen in a sitting position, using a stool or an unpadded chair with a straight back. Sit slightly forward on the chair so that you are not tempted to rest your back on it. Your feet should be flat on the floor, with your knees bent at right angles. Rest your hands in your lap or on your thighs. Try to keep your head balanced on top of your spine, with your shoulders, neck, and abdominal muscles relaxed; try not to let yourself slump backwards or forwards.

Place your chair or cushion so that you are facing a blank wall. There must be nothing that you

ZAZEN

Sitting in a cross-legged position, count your breaths in cycles of 1 to 10, keeping your mind clear of other thoughts.

can focus your mind on. When you are settled and relaxed, focus your attention on your breathing. Keeping your eyes open and your mind clear, begin to count your breaths until you reach 10, and then begin again at one. If your mind becomes distracted and you lose count, settle yourself once again and resume the count at one. Continue for 20 minutes, timing yourself with an alarm. After the alarm sounds, spend 10 minutes walking around the room in a circle, to get the blood flowing in your legs. Continue meditating as you walk, counting your breaths. Return to your seat for a second round of 20 minutes of sitting followed by 10 minutes of walking.

The difficulty of zazen is its simplicity. In other forms of meditation, the student is asked to repeat a mantra (a kind of prayer) or to concentrate on a complex geometrical pattern such as a mandala (a Hindu or Buddhist graphic symbol of the universe), to aid concentration. In zazen, however, the student has only a blank wall and his or her own breathing to focus upon.

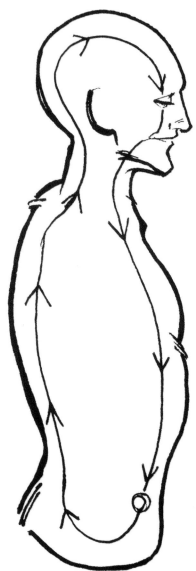

Imagine the chi flowing in a loop from the top of your head, down your front, and up your back.

DAOISM

Daoism is the second major religion of China after Buddhism. The Book of the Way expounds the philosophy of Daoism. It teaches that humans can only be truly happy if they live in harmony with the Tao ("the Way"), and if the two qualities of yin and yang are balanced in their lives.

There is a branch of Daoism in which the main concern is the search for immortality. This is usually taken to mean the spiritual immortality of the soul after the death of the body, but the ancient Chinese believed that they could find physical immortality through a combination of diet, exercise, magical rituals, and a special immortality elixir. One emperor was so obsessed by the search for eternal life that he drank molten gold with unfortunate, but rather predictable, results.

THE CIRCULATION OF CHI EXERCISE

We have already seen some basic types of energy work in the "raising chi" and chi gung exercises (see pp. 39–49). The "circulation of chi" exercise is adapted from Daoist practice, and was probably influenced by the Indian pranayama (Sanskrit for breath, life energy, and control), which are breathing exercises that are taught in the yoga system of exercise.

To perform the "circulation of chi" exercise, sit in a meditative pose that will enable you to keep your head and back erect. If you have trouble remaining in a cross-legged or kneeling pose, practice in a sitting position, using a stool or a chair, as in the zazen meditation (pp. 85–86). Imagine a channel running from your nose, down the front of your body, to the dantian energy center two inches (5 cm) below your navel, and down and around to the base of your spine. The channel climbs along your spine until it reaches the crown of your head, where it loops once more down to your nose.

As you breathe in, chi enters your nose and begins to flow down the front of the channel to the dantian. Instead of letting it accumulate there, however, as in the "raising chi" exercise (see pp. 39–42), move the chi around the channel and then to the top of your head and back to your nose. The next breath will add even more chi to that which is already circulating, making it concentrated, more dense, and heavier to move. The light and heat that the chi gives off also increase.

REPETITION

In the film *The Karate Kid,* the sensei teaches his student the basic moves of his fighting art by making him repeat simple moves. He makes him practice "painting the fence" and "waxing the car" over and over again, until his body has learned to do the movements without reference to his brain. The kata and drill practices used by many of the martial arts have the same purpose. In an attack situation, a trained person can respond instantly—infinitely faster than if he or she had to think his or her moves out one at a time.

VISUALIZATION

Another powerful martial arts training technique now employed by professional athletes is visualization, a form of mental rehearsal for a match or race. This is similar to practicing forms, only you do not actually perform the moves. By visualizing yourself performing certain practice drills of combinations, however, you are ensuring that your mind is participating in your martial arts training just as much as your body is.

Repetition is one of the key teaching techniques in the martial arts. Taekwondo students drill in kata in perfect unison, their movements effortlessly synchronized.

Mental rehearsal is especially useful when training for a swimming, cycling, or running race, when the variables (such as distance and terrain) are known.

If your goal is to increase and maintain overall fitness, martial arts offers a way to get there. You'll increase your physical stamina, strength, and flexibility. And in many cases, you'll add to your mental health and sense of well-being. This will not be an easy road, but by following the example of other students and teachers, you'll make it. As with any experience, the more you put into it, the more you'll get out of it.

GLOSSARY

Acupuncture Chinese medical art in which needles are inserted in the meridians to control the flow of chi

Bout Free-sparring match in the martial arts; these can be no- or full-contact

Chi/qi Cosmic energy believed by the Chinese to animate all matter; humans acquire chi from food and from the environment; in the soft/internal martial arts, chi is used as a weapon

Chi gung (Chinese: energy work; also qi gung); techniques designed to increase and control the chi in the body to improve health and fitness

Dantian Main reservoir of chi in the human body, located two inches (5 cm) below the navel

Dojo Training hall used for all Japanese martial arts

Herbalism Chinese medical art in which natural products, such as herbs and minerals, are given to patients to control or stimulate the flow of chi

Karate-ka A student of karate-do, the art of the empty hand

Kata (Japanese: form); a sequence of exercises used to teach the basic moves of karate-do

Ki Japanese word for chi

Kiai (Japanese: vocalization of ki); a shout used in karate during an attack to unsettle an opponent and also project one's ki into the movement

Kumite	Non-contact free sparring in karate-do
Pacifism	Philosophy of nonviolence that rejects war between states; the most famous modern representative of pacifism was Mahatma Gandhi
Satori	(Japanese: awakening); enlightenment desired by students of Zen Buddhism; this can be a sudden event, or one achieved after many years of meditation
Samurai	Japanese warrior of the 12th–17th centuries
Seiza	(Japanese: correct sitting); kneeling pose used in Japan for meditation as well as formal occasions
Tatami	Woven straw mat used as flooring in traditional Japanese houses and dojo
Tonfa	Short poles featuring side handles, like modern-day police batons
Walking meditation	Short period of walking during a Zen meditation to loosen the limbs after sitting meditation (or zazen)
Yang/Yin	The two energies that make up the universe in Chinese Daoist thought; yang is the light, masculine, active energy; yin is the dark, feminine, passive energy
Zendo	Meditation hall in a Japanese Zen monastery or temple

Clothing and Equipment

Clothing

Gi: The gi is the most typical martial arts "uniform." Usually in white, but also available in other colors, it consists of a cotton thigh-length jacket and calf-length trousers. Gis come in three weights: light, medium, and heavy. Lightweight gis are cooler than heavyweight gis, but not as strong. The jacket is usually bound at the waist with a belt.

Belt: Belts are used in the martial arts to denote the rank and experience of the wearer. They are made from strong linen or cotton and wrap several times around the body before tying. Beginners usually wear a white belt, and the final belt is almost always black.

Hakama: A long folded skirt with five pleats at the front and one at the back. It is a traditional form of clothing in kendo, iaido, and jujutsu.

Zori: A simple pair of slip-on sandals worn in the dojo when not training to keep the floor clean.

Training Aids

Mook yan jong: A wooden dummy against which the martial artist practices his blocks and punches and conditions his limbs for combat.

Makiwara: A plank of wood set in the ground used for punching and kicking practice.

Focus pads: Circular pads worn on the hands by one person, while his or her partner uses the pads for training accurate punching.

PROTECTIVE EQUIPMENT

Headguard: A padded, protective helmet that protects the wearer from blows to the face and head.

Joint supports: Tight foam or bandage sleeves that go around elbow, knee, or ankle joints and protect the muscles and joints against damage during training.

Groin protector: A well-padded undergarment for men that protects the testicles and the abdomen from kicks and low punches.

Practice mitts: Lightweight boxing gloves that protect the wearer's hands from damage in sparring, and reduce the risk of cuts being inflicted on the opponent.

Chest protector: A sturdy shield worn by women over the chest to protect the breasts during sparring.

FURTHER READING

Barnes, J. *Power Training for Combat, MMA, Boxing, Wrestling, Martial Arts, and Self-Defense: How to Develop Knockout Punching Power, etc.* Fitness Learning, 2013.

Chou, Lily. *The Martial Artist's Book of Yoga.* Ulysses Press: 2013.

Edd, Al Gotay. *Martial Arts Basics: From Olympic Sports to Self-Defense Systems.* Outskirts Press: 2013

McKenzie, Martin and Stefanie Kirchner. *Total Knockout Fitness.* Human Kinetics: 2014.

SERIES CONSULTANT

Adam James is the Founder of Rainbow Warrior Martial Arts and the Director for the National College of Exercise Professionals. Adam is a 10th Level Instructor of Wei Kuen Do, Chi Fung, and Modern Escrima, and a 5th Degree Black Belt in Kempo, Karate, Juijitsu, and Kobudo. He is also the co-creator of the NCEP-Rainbow Warrior Martial Arts MMA Trainer certification program, which has been endorsed by the Commissioner of MMA for the State of Hawaii and by the U.S. Veterans Administration. Adam was also the Director of World Black Belt, whose Founding Members include Chuck Norris, Bob Wall, Gene LeBell, and 50 of the world's greatest martial artists. In addition, Adam is an actor, writer and filmmaker, and he has performed with Andy Garcia, Tommy Lee Jones, and Steven Seagal. As a writer, he has been published in numerous martial arts books and magazines, including *Black Belt*, *Masters Magazine*, and the *Journal of Asian Martial Arts*, and he has written several feature film screenplays.

USEFUL WEB SITES

http://www.stadion.com
A publishing company with a specialty in sports fitness.

http://www.nestacertified.com
Information on training to be a personal trainer or how to find trainers near you.

www.blackbeltmag.com/category/daily/martial-arts-fitness
A leading martial arts magazine offers a clearinghouse of information on martial arts and fitness.

Publisher's Note: The websites listed on this page were active at the time of publication. The publisher is not responsible for websites that have changed their address or discontinued operation since the date of publication. The publisher reviews and updates the websites each time the book is reprinted.

ABOUT THE AUTHOR

Eric Chaline is a personal-training consultant and health and fitness journalist and author with credentials in the martial arts, Zen Buddhism and yoga. After graduating from Cambridge University and the School of Oriental and African Studies in London, he studied in Japan at Osaka Foreign Studies University, where he pursued his interests in Japanese history, philosophy, and the martial arts. He remained in Japan after completing his studies and supervised the English-language martial arts publications of a major Japanese publisher, which included books on aikido by the current doshu, Ueshiba Morihei, and on kyudo, Japanese archery.

INDEX

References in italics refer to illustration captions

aerobic fitness 9
agility 12, *13*
aikido 20
    belts 22
    preventing injury 75–81
athletes, professional *22, 23*
automatic-movement
        exercise 48–9

back kick 66, *68*
backwards break-fall *77,*
        78–9
balance 9, 12, *13,* 51
basic stretching program
        29–33
belts 20, *23*
bicep stretch 33
Bodhidharma 15–16, *17*
Book of the Way, The 86–7
box splits 73
break-falls 77–81
breathing control *34, 43, 85,*
        87–8
Buddhism 14–16, *17,* 83–7
butterfly, the 72–3

calves stretch 31–2
capoeira 18
Carradine, David 16
Chang San Feng 36
Chen Chia Kou 36
chi 12
    energy work 35–49
    mental training *86,* 87–8
    pushing-hands 56
    and the West 14
chi gung 35, 42–9
choosing a martial art 18–23
circuit training 71–3
"circulation of chi" exercise
        87–8
clothing 12, 20, 22, *23,* 26
"cloud hands" *47*
combinations 70
consulting a doctor 11
coordination 9, 12, 51

dantian 39
Daoism 25, 36, 83, 86–7
Dhyana 15
doctors, consulting 11
dojos 19, 22
dress 12, 20, 22,*23,* 26
drills *54,* 69–70, 81
dynamic stances 55–6

Eastern training methods
        9–23
endurance 51–7
energy work 35–49

feng shui 14
flexibility 9, 12, *13*
"forms" 88
forward bend *70,* 71–2
forwards break-fall 79
Four Noble Truths 14
free-sparring *57*
front kick 65–76
front stance 52, *53*

gi 22
grading exams 77

hamstring stretch 30, *32*
head rolling 26–7
history of the martial arts
        14–17
holding stances 55
horse stance 52, *53,* 69
hsing-i 37

I-Ching 37
iaido 23, 84
immortality 87
injury prevention 75–81

Jigoro, Kano 75
judo 18
    belts 22
    first judo school 20
    preventing injury 75–81
jujutsu 16, 75

karate 16, 18
    belts 22
    sparring *10*
    stance 51
    strength and stamina
        59–73
    teaching style 19–20
Karate Kid 88
kata 60, *61–73*
kendo 23, 84
kickboxing 18, 75
kicking techniques 65–9

knee circles 29
kumite 60
kung fu *13*
KungFu (TV program) 16
kyudo 23, 84

Lee, Bruce 10, 19, *59*
location, for training 12
lunge punch 62–3
lunges 72

Man, Yip 19
mats 78
meditation 84, 85–6
mental concentration *51*
mental training 82–9
Morihei, Ueshiba 75
muscular endurance 51–7

Okinawate 59–61
one-leg stance *53,* 55
"opening the chest" *44*

pa-kua 37
partner work 51, *54,* 56
pentjak-silat 18
posture *34, 38,* 51–7
pranayama 87–8
preparation 25–33
preventing injury 75–81
punching techniques 62–5
"pushing-hands" exercises
        51, *54,* 56
push-ups 71
"pushing palms while
        turning waist" *46*

qi 12
    energy work 35–49
    mental training *86,* 87–8
    and the West 14
quadriceps stretch 30–31

"raising chi" 39–42
rear stance 52–5, *57*
repetition 88–9
reverse punch *64,* 65
rollout *80,* 81
roundhouse kick 67–9
runner's stretch 30–31

safety, consulting a doctor 11
samurai 75
satori 83
"scooping the sea while
        looking at the sky"
        48–9
"separating the clouds" *45*
Shaolin lohan 16, 51

shoes, for training 12
short warm-up program
        26–9
Shotokan karate 20, 60
shoulder rolls 27–8
Siddharta, Prince Gautama
        14
side kick 66–7, *68*
sideways break-fall *78,* 79
Simplified Beijing Form 37
sparring *57*
speed 9, *13,* 51
spine stretch 33
spiritual training 82–9
stamina 12, *13*
stance 51–7
strength 9, 10, 12, *13,* 58–73
stretching program 29–33

taekwondo *8,* 16
t'ai chi ch'uan
    athletes and 23
    energy work 36–49
    forms 59
    pushing-hands 56
    recognized by Chinese
        government 21
Tamo 15–16
Taoism 25, 36, 83, 86–7
tatami mats 78
teaching styles 19–23
Thai kickboxing 18, *75*
Traditional Chinese
        Medicine (TCM) 14
training
    mental 82–9
    physical 9–23
Triads 20
triceps stretch 32

"up-and-over drill" 81

visualization 89

waist rotations 28
walking meditation 84, 86
warming up 25–33
where to train 12
which martial art? 18–23
wing chun 18, 19, *21*

Yang Lu Chan 36

zazen meditation 84, 85–6
Zen Buddhism 83–6

Renbrook School

The Alan N. Houghton Library

Amazing
Poisonous
Animals

EYEWITNESS JUNIORS

Amazing Poisonous Animals

WRITTEN BY
ALEXANDRA PARSONS

PHOTOGRAPHED BY
JERRY YOUNG

ALFRED A. KNOPF • NEW YORK

Conceived and produced by
Dorling Kindersley Limited

Editor Scott Steedman
Senior art editor Jacquie Gulliver
Managing editor Sophie Mitchell
Editorial director Sue Unstead
Art director Colin Walton

Special photography by Jerry Young
Illustrations by Mark Iley, John Bendall-Brunello, and John Hutchinson
Animals supplied by Trevor Smith's Animal World
Editorial consultants The staff of the Natural History Museum, London

This is a Borzoi Book published by Alfred A. Knopf, Inc.

First American edition, 1990

Manufactured in Italy   0 9 8 7 6 5 4

Library of Congress Cataloging in Publication Data
Parsons, Alexandra
Amazing poisonous animals / written by Alexandra Parsons;
photographs by Jerry Young.
p. cm. — (Eyewitness juniors; 8)
Summary: Text and photographs introduce poisonous animals such
as the fire salamander, death puffer, gila monster, and sea anemone.
1. Poisonous animals — Juvenile literature. [1. Poisonous animals.]
I. Young, Jerry, ill. II. Title. III. Series.
QL100.P36   1990   591.6'9 — dc20   90-31883
ISBN   0-679-80699-7
ISBN   0-679-90699-1 (lib. bdg.)

Color reproduction by Colourscan, Singapore
Typeset by Windsorgraphics, Ringwood, Hampshire
Printed in Italy by A. Mondadori Editore, Verona

Contents

Why be poisonous? 8

Arrow-poison frog 10

Deadly adder 12

Stinging tentacles 14

Fiery salamanders 16

Death puffer 18

Vicious fishes 20

Toxic toad 22

Gardener's surprise 24

Desert monster 26

Stings with wings 28

Index 29

Why be poisonous?

All animals have to find food and keep out of the way of other hungry animals. Some of them succeed by running fast; others have claws or horns or are good at hiding and keeping still. The animals in this book use another tactic: they make poison, giving their enemies some nasty surprises.

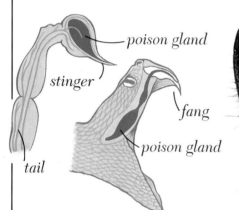

poison gland

stinger

tail

fang

poison gland

The scorpion makes a warning noise by rubbing its claws against its legs

A bite or a sting?

Animals are poisonous in different ways. Scorpions inject poison into their victims with special stingers on their tails. Snakes bite and inject poison with their fangs.

What are poisons and venom?

Any chemical that can harm or kill another living creature is a poison. Poisons that are made by animals may also be called venom.

stinger at end of tail

The imperial scorpion

The imperial scorpion (above) can be 5 inches long. It stings only if it is stepped on, or if it catches an animal that is too big to kill with its claws.

A sting in its tail

The scorpion hunts in the leaves and bark on the forest floor. It has big claws like a crab for grabbing insects. It arches its tail over its back, stinger quivering, and then it's goodbye, grasshopper!

Hell's angels

Snakes, spiders, and scorpions have always been symbols of evil. The Egyptians worshipped the cobra, and some people have scorpions tattooed on their bodies.

Shall we waltz?

When scorpions court, they take one another by the claws and dance.

A poisonous kick

There are no poisonous birds anywhere in the world. But there are a few poisonous mammals, such as the male platypus, which has poisonous claws on its ankles.

Small but deadly

Most poisonous animals are small. This little centipede could kill a mouse or a toad with one nip from its poisonous claws.

9

Arrow-poison frog

These tiny frogs live in the rain forests of South and Central America. Their bright and beautiful colors say one thing – Don't eat me, I'm poisonous!

The most deadly poison made by an animal...

....comes from the skin of the golden arrow-poison frog. One tiny frog the size of your thumb carries enough poison to kill 20,000 mice.

Terrible frog
This frog has no name in English. But its scientific name means terrible arrow-poison frog!

Poison for arrows
South American Indians dip their arrows in frog poison. Once a monkey or a jaguar has been scratched with a poisoned arrow, the hunters follow it through the jungle waiting for it to collapse and die.

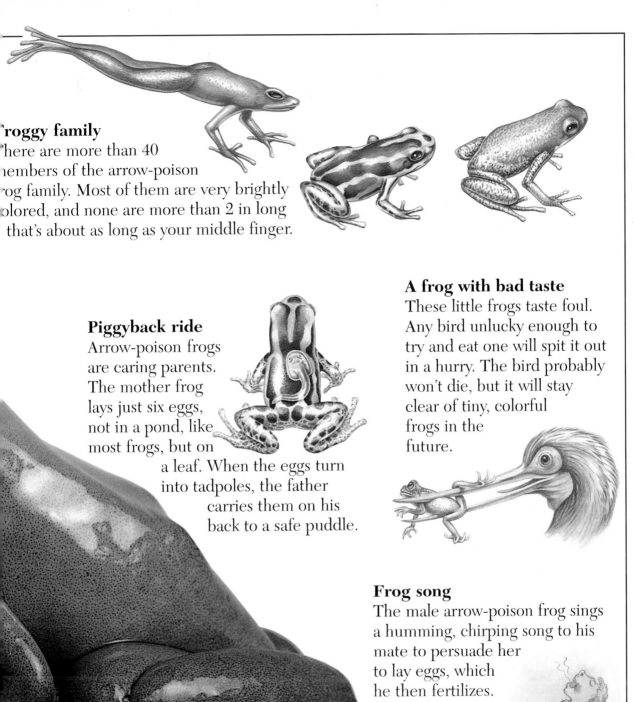

Froggy family

There are more than 40 members of the arrow-poison frog family. Most of them are very brightly colored, and none are more than 2 in long – that's about as long as your middle finger.

Piggyback ride

Arrow-poison frogs are caring parents. The mother frog lays just six eggs, not in a pond, like most frogs, but on a leaf. When the eggs turn into tadpoles, the father carries them on his back to a safe puddle.

A frog with bad taste

These little frogs taste foul. Any bird unlucky enough to try and eat one will spit it out in a hurry. The bird probably won't die, but it will stay clear of tiny, colorful frogs in the future.

Frog song

The male arrow-poison frog sings a humming, chirping song to his mate to persuade her to lay eggs, which he then fertilizes.

Deadly adder

The African puff adder is one of the world's deadliest snakes. It spends most of its time snoozing in the sand, waiting for an animal to stumble by. Then it strikes with amazing speed and sinks in its deadly poisonous fangs.

A gruesome way to die

The puff adder's poison makes its victim bleed on the inside. At first there is a burning pain around the wound. Then a huge bruise appears and the victim's lips begin to tingle. The poison can be fatal within half an hour or a few days.

layer of fake "skin"

fang

A splash in your tea?

Milking a puff adder is a little more dangerous than milking a cow. The idea is to make the snake bite a fake piece of "skin" so it will squirt its poison into a jar.

The poison is then used to make a puff adder antivenin, a special liquid for curing people who have been bitten by puff adders.

Colors blend in with desert sands

The Devil's poison
In one version of the Garden of Eden story, the Devil hides inside a snake's tooth. When the snake opens its mouth, out come the poisonous words of the Devil. He persuades Eve to bite the apple and commit the first sin.

Fangs a lot!
The puff adder has long fangs. But they're not quite as impressive as the fangs of the Gaboon viper (above), which can be 2 inches long.

Live ammunition
Roman admirals were known to throw jars of live poisonous snakes into their enemies' ships.

13

Stinging tentacles

The sea anemone looks like an underwater flower. But it is really an animal, with poisonous tentacles instead of petals. It uses its tentacles to paralyze fish and drag them into its huge mouth.

Fumbling for food

The anemone is always groping around with its tentacles. Each one is lined with thousands of tiny stinging cells, just waiting for a big fish or a big toe to come their way.

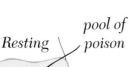

Resting

pool of poison

Whips of poison

When a fish touches a tentacle, the anemone's stinging cells are triggered. A tiny whip covered in barbs and poison comes lashing out of each cell.

barb

Triggered

Meet my friend

The clown fish (right) is not hurt by the anemone's poison. The two help each other to survive. The fish cleans the anemone and shares some of its food with it. In exchange the anemone lets the fish hide in its tentacles.

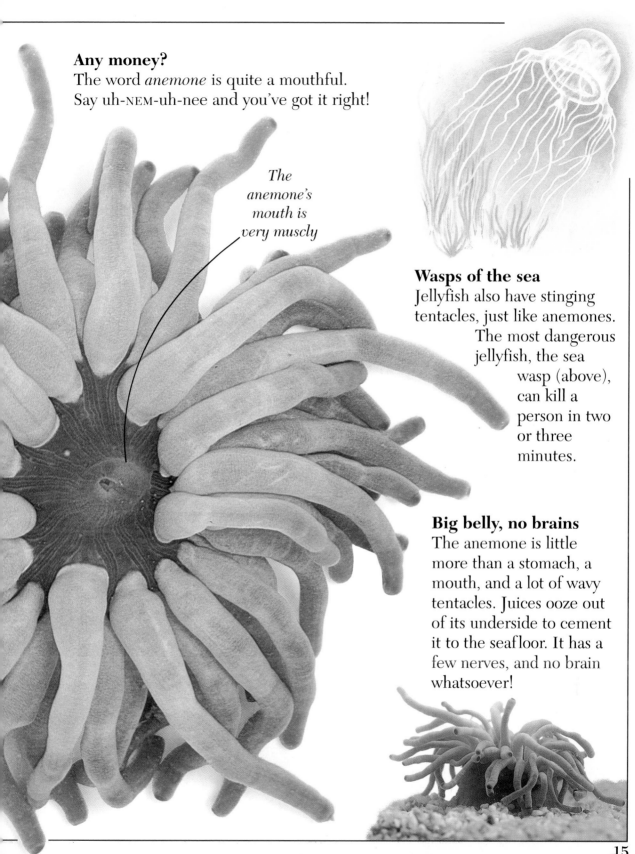

Any money?
The word *anemone* is quite a mouthful.
Say uh-NEM-uh-nee and you've got it right!

The anemone's mouth is very muscly

Wasps of the sea
Jellyfish also have stinging tentacles, just like anemones. The most dangerous jellyfish, the sea wasp (above), can kill a person in two or three minutes.

Big belly, no brains
The anemone is little more than a stomach, a mouth, and a lot of wavy tentacles. Juices ooze out of its underside to cement it to the seafloor. It has a few nerves, and no brain whatsoever!

Fiery salamanders

Birds, snakes, and shrews would all like a slice of salamander for supper. So these tiny animals have developed some nasty poisons to save their skin. And that's exactly where they store the poisons – in their skin.

Pretending to be poisonous

Some harmless animals have the same bright colors as deadly ones, so that predators leave them alone too. The red salamander looks just like the young of the deadly red-spotted newt, but it hasn't got a drop of poison in its body.

Red salamander

Salamanders from different places have different patterns of yellow and black

Young red-spotted newt

Not for hunting

Salamanders use their poison only for defense. When hunting, they rely on surprise and a quick bite.

poison gland

Fire salamander

The poison of this animal (above) won't kill you, but it would sting if it got into a cut. And birds don't seem to like the taste much.

Rib tickler
The spiny newt (right) has poison glands at the tips of its ribs. When the newt is squeezed in a bird's beak, the ribs burst the glands and squirt poison into the bird's mouth.

Skin on body and tail is full of poison

Fire extinguisher
People once believed that the salamander was a magic animal that lived and danced in fire. Stories were even told of salamanders putting out fires, but the stories are not true.

The California newt
The flesh and eggs of this little creature (right) are full of a deadly nerve poison. It is so powerful that just one drop will kill 7,000 mice.

Between land and water
Salamanders and their close relatives newts are amphibians (am-FIB-ee-uns). This means that they can live both in the water and on the land. Some amphibians never leave their ponds, but others (like fire salamanders) hardly ever get their feet wet.

Death puffer

This tropical fish looks pretty harmless. But in its body is a poison more deadly than any snake venom. The poison can kill people in half an hour, by attacking their nerves so they can't move or breathe properly.

Lazy days

The death puffer swims slow and is easy to catch. It is onl dangerous if it is eaten witho being prepared correctly.

Huff and puff

There are over a hundred kinds of pufferfish, and all of them have the same amazing talent. When they sense danger, they suck in water and blow themselves up like balloons.

Deadly dish

The Japanese are very fond of death puffer, which they call *fugu*. Chefs are specially trained to cut away the poisonous parts of the fish. But every year about 20 people collapse and die from *fugu* poisoning.

Blue-ringed octopus

This octopus (right) is one of the deadliest creatures in the sea. It injects its victim with a huge dose of TTX – the same poison found in the death puffer.

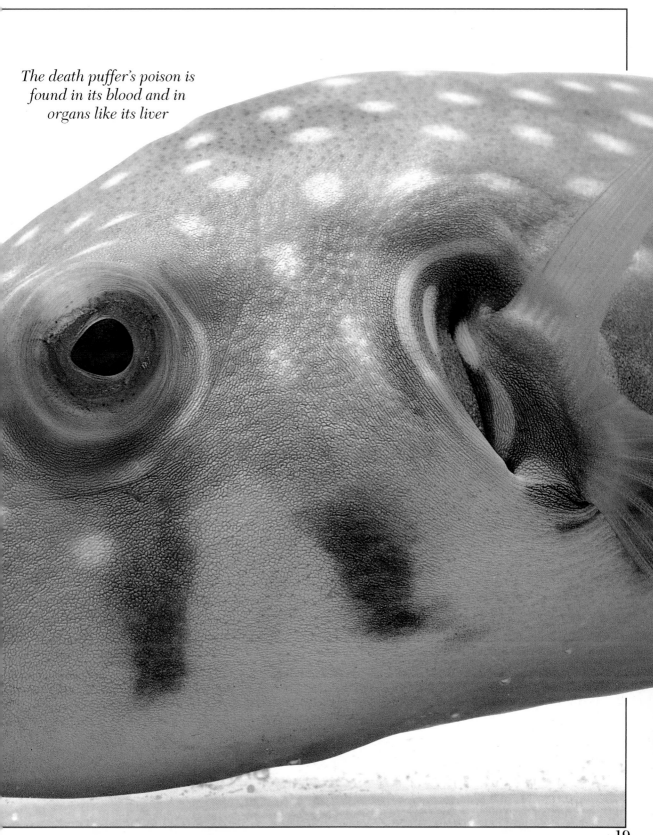

The death puffer's poison is found in its blood and in organs like its liver

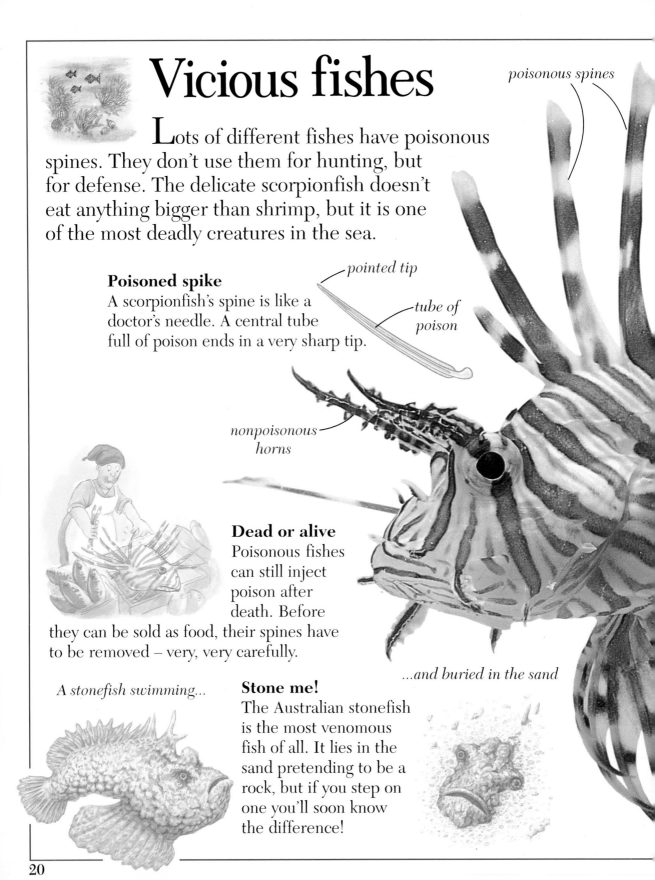

Vicious fishes

Lots of different fishes have poisonous spines. They don't use them for hunting, but for defense. The delicate scorpionfish doesn't eat anything bigger than shrimp, but it is one of the most deadly creatures in the sea.

poisonous spines

Poisoned spike
A scorpionfish's spine is like a doctor's needle. A central tube full of poison ends in a very sharp tip.

pointed tip

tube of poison

nonpoisonous horns

Dead or alive
Poisonous fishes can still inject poison after death. Before they can be sold as food, their spines have to be removed – very, very carefully.

...and buried in the sand

A stonefish swimming...

Stone me!
The Australian stonefish is the most venomous fish of all. It lies in the sand pretending to be a rock, but if you step on one you'll soon know the difference!

A sting from this beautiful scorpionfish can cause great pain

Saving energy
The scorpionfish (left) is found in warm, tropical seas. It glides along lazily, safe in the knowledge that bigger animals will let it be.

Open wide
Stingrays have been famous for their poison for thousands of years. The Romans even used their stings to stop toothaches.

stinger

Toxic toad

All toads are poisonous, and the giant toad is the biggest, ugliest, and and most dangerous of all. It uses the warty lumps on its shoulders to poison any animal that attacks it.

What an appetite!
Giant toads originally came from the Americas, but now they are found in Hawaii and Australia. Wherever they are they eat huge numbers of beetles, spiders, and anything else they can cram into their mouths.

A big mistake
Australian farmers imported giant toads to eat beetles that were destroying their sugar cane. The toads ate some beetles, but they also ate up everything else. Now they are a bigger problem than the beetles ever were!

Shoulder pads
A toad's poison glands bulge out around its head and look like shoulder pads. A cat or dog that ate a toad would get a mouthful of poison – and might die in an hour.

swollen poison glands

All toads have four toes on their front feet and five on the back

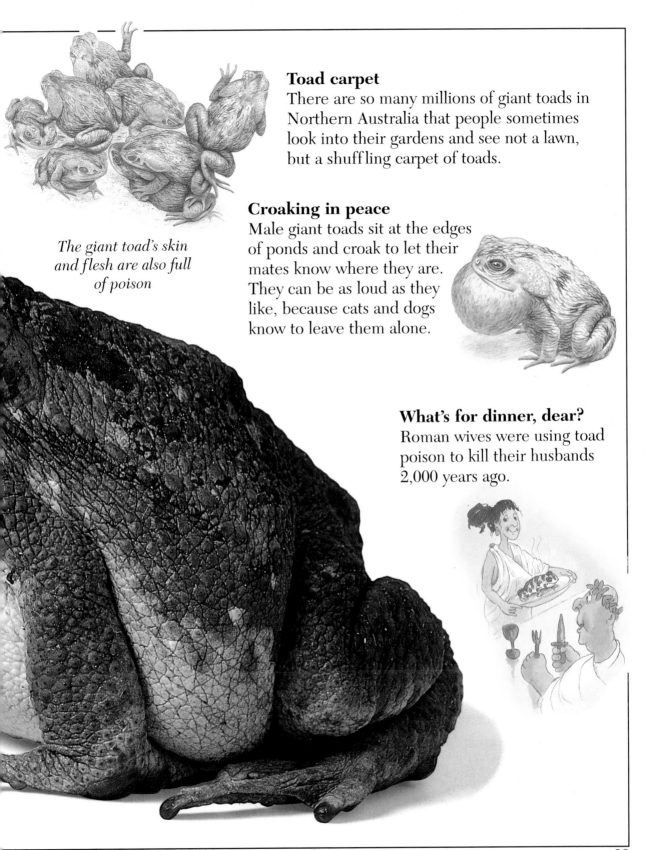

Toad carpet

There are so many millions of giant toads in Northern Australia that people sometimes look into their gardens and see not a lawn, but a shuffling carpet of toads.

The giant toad's skin and flesh are also full of poison

Croaking in peace

Male giant toads sit at the edges of ponds and croak to let their mates know where they are. They can be as loud as they like, because cats and dogs know to leave them alone.

What's for dinner, dear?

Roman wives were using toad poison to kill their husbands 2,000 years ago.

Gardener's surprise

All spiders bite, and all of them are poisonous. But some are nastier than others. The venom of the Australian funnel-web, which digs its den in people's gardens, can kill a person in less than two hours.

Injecting the poison
A spider's fangs are connected to glands bulging with poison. When the spider bites, it sinks in its fangs and gets a good grip with the help of special "teeth." Then it pumps its victim full of venom.

fang *tube*

poison gland

"teeth"

Giant killer
Most spiders eat insects, but funnel-webs have been known to prey on lizards and small birds.

A bad case of the blues
A nip from the funnel-web causes pain, cramps, and heavy sweating. Then the victim turns blue, froths at the mouth, and soon dies. In 1980 an antivenin was developed.

Don't worry

There are 30,000 kinds of spiders, and the funnel-web is one of only about 10 that are known to kill people.

Comfortable nest

The female funnel-web lays up to 250 eggs. She drops them straight into a cocoon, like a tiny silk pillow, at the bottom of her burrow.

A close family

Baby spiders are called spiderlings. Hundreds are born, but only a few make it to adulthood – often by eating their own brothers and sisters.

All spiders have eight legs – unlike insects, which have six

Don't look back

The most feared spider in the world is the black widow (right). Its bite causes horrible pain, dizziness, and death. And it has the troublesome habit of spinning its web across toilet seats!

Desert monster

There are only two kinds of poisonous lizards in the world, and this is one of them. It is called the Gila monster and it lives in the deserts of the United States.

Hello, cowboy!
This big, slow-moving lizard is named after the Gila (HEE-luh) River basin in Arizona.

A monstrous display
When a Gila monster feels threatened, it throws its head in the air and snorts and puffs like crazy. Its poison is mainly used for hunting, and sometimes in self-defense.

Brightly patterned skin warns other animals to stay away

*strong claws for
digging burrows*

Fat tail
There isn't much to eat in
hot, sandy deserts. So the
Gila monster has to eat as
much as it can whenever
it can. It stores fat in its
tail and can live off this
for months or even years.

roovy teeth
ne monster's poison spills into
mouth from a gland in its
ttom jaw. The lizard uses its
ecial grooved teeth to chew
e poison
to its victim.

groove

Tooth

*Bottom
jaw*

poison gland

Immunized
Many poisonous animals
are immune to their own
poison. This means that
they can be bitten by another
of their kind – or even bite
themselves – without being
poisoned.

Paralyzing poison
Drop for drop, a Gila monster's
poison is more deadly than a
rattlesnake's. It attacks the
nerves and causes horrible pain
and paralysis. Luckily, the
monster rarely injects enough
poison to kill a person.

Southern cousin
The only other poisonous lizard is
the Gila monster's closest relative,
the beaded lizard from Mexico (right).

Stings with wings

Bees and wasps are the poisonous animals you're most likely to meet. Usually their stings just hurt for a while. But a very few people are allergic to wasp or bee poison and can die from a single sting.

Domestic honeyb

The bee

Where would we be without bees? They fly from flower to flower, collecting nectar to make into honey. On their voyages they carry pollen from one flower to the next, which guarantees that fruits will grow from the flowers.

Wasps

Despite their nasty stings, wasps are also useful animal because they kill a lot o insects that destroy plants and fru

This European wasp is one of at least 50,000 different kinds of wasp

Swarming

Bees live together in nests. When one nest splits into two, a huge cloud of bees leaves their home in search of a good spot to build a new one. This cloud of bees is called a swarm.

Stung to death

A honeybee's sting and poison sac are in its tail. When it stings a person, its barbed sting gets stuck in the skin. The sting and sac are ripped off and stay in the victim, pumping poison while the bee goes off to die.

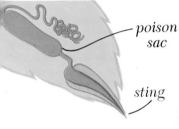

poison sac

sting

Killer bees

A normal bee sting won't kill you. One boy was stung 2,243 times by an angry swarm and survived! But a new bee from South America has killed more than 150 people.

Spider slayer

Bees are vegetarians, but wasps are aggressive hunters that often attack bigger animals. A few kinds even kill and eat spiders.

Index

amphibians 17
antivenin 12, 25
arrow-poison frog 10-11

beaded lizard 27
bee 28-29
birds 9, 11, 16
black widow spider 25
blue-ringed octopus 18

California newt 17
camouflage 12
cane toad 22-23
centipede 9
claws 8, 9, 27
courting 9, 11, 23

death puffer 18-19

fangs 8, 12, 13, 24
fire salamander 16-17
fugu 18
funnel-web spider 24-25

Garden of Eden 13
Gila monster 26-27

jellyfish 15

killer bee 29

immunity 27

platypus 9
poison glands 8, 16, 22, 24, 27, 29
puff adder 12-13
pufferfish 18-19

salamanders 16-17
scorpion 8-9
scorpionfish 20-21
sea anemone 14-15
sea wasp 15
snake, milking of 12
snakes 8, 9, 12, 13, 27
spiders 9, 22, 24-25
stingray 20
stings 8, 9, 14, 15, 29
stonefish 21
swarming 29

tentacles 14, 15

wasp 28-29